Working Papers
Volume 1, Chapters 1-12

for use with

Fundamental Accounting Principles

Seventeenth Edition

Kermit D. Larson
University of Texas at Austin

John J. Wild
University of Wisconsin at Madison

Barbara Chiappetta
Nassau Community College

 **McGraw-Hill**
Irwin

Boston   Burr Ridge, IL   Dubuque, IA   Madison, WI   New York   San Francisco   St. Louis
Bangkok   Bogotá   Caracas   Kuala Lumpur   Lisbon   London   Madrid   Mexico City
Milan   Montreal   New Delhi   Santiago   Seoul   Singapore   Sydney   Taipei   Toronto

Working Papers, Volume 1, Chapters 1-12 for use with
FUNDAMENTAL ACCOUNTING PRINCIPLES
Kermit D. Larson, John J. Wild, and Barbara Chiappetta

Published by McGraw-Hill/Irwin, an imprint of The McGraw-Hill Companies, Inc., 1221 Avenue of the
Americas, New York, NY 10020. Copyright © 2005, 2002, 1999, 1996, 1993, 1990
by The McGraw-Hill Companies, Inc. All rights reserved.

1 2 3 4 5 6 7 8 9 0 CUS/CUS 0 9 8 7 6 5 4

ISBN 0-07-286985-2

www.mhhe.com

The McGraw-Hill Companies

Table of Contents

(a) _____   (g) _____
(b) _____   (h) _____
(c) _____   (i) _____
(d) _____   (j) _____
(e) _____   (k) _____
(f) _____   (l) _____

Quick Study 1-2

(a)

GAAP: _____

Importance: _____

_____

_____

_____

SEC: _____

Importance: _____

_____

_____

_____

FASB: _____

Importance: _____

_____

_____

_____

(b) _____

_____

_____

_____

_____

Quick Study 1-3

(1) _____

_____

_____

(2) _____

_____

_____

(3) _____

_____

_____

_____

_____

Name _____

_____
_____
_____
_____
_____
_____

Quick Study 1-5

Business transactions: _____
_____
_____

Business events: _____
_____
_____
_____

Quick Study 1-6

_____
_____
_____
_____

Quick Study 1-7

(a) _____
(b) _____
(c) _____

Quick Study 1-8

(a) _____
_____

(b) _____
_____
_____

Quick Study 1-9

Assets	=	Liabilities	+	Equity
$ 30,000		(a) _____		$20,000
(b) _____		$50,000		$30,000
$ 90,000		$10,000		(c) _____

Name _____

(a) (1) _____

   (2) _____

   (3) _____

(b)	Assets	=	Liabilities	+	Equity
		=		+	

Quick Study 1-11

(a) _____ **(d)** _____ **(g)** _____

(b) _____ **(e)** _____ **(h)** _____

(c) _____ **(f)** _____ **(i)** _____

Quick Study 1-12

Return on Assets: _____

_____

_____

Interpretation: _____

_____

_____

(a) _____

(b) _____

(c) _____

(d) _____

(e) _____

(f) _____

(g) _____

Exercise 1-2

(1) _____

(2) _____

(3) _____

(4) _____

(5) _____

(6) _____

(7) _____

Exercise 1-3

(1) _____

(2) _____

(3) _____

(4) _____

(5) _____

(6) _____

(7) _____

(8) _____

Exercise 1-4

External User:	
	_____
	_____
	_____
External User:	
	_____
	_____
	_____
External User:	
	_____
	_____
	_____

Chapter 1   Exercise 1-5   *Name* _____

(a) _____

_____

_____

(b) _____

_____

_____

(c) _____

_____

_____

(d) _____

_____

_____

_____

Exercise 1-6

(1) _____

(2) _____

(3) _____

(4) _____

(5) _____

(a) _____
_____
_____
_____
_____

(b) _____
_____
_____
_____
_____
_____
_____
_____
_____

(c) _____
_____
_____
_____
_____
_____
_____
_____

Exercise 1-8

	Assets	=	Liabilities	+	Equity	
(a)						
(b)						
(c)						

(a) _____

_____

(b) _____

_____

(c) _____

_____

(d) _____

_____

(e) _____

_____

(f) _____

_____

(g) _____

_____

Exercise 1-10

(a) _____

_____

(b) _____

_____

(c) _____

_____

(d) _____

_____

(e) _____

_____

(a) _____

_____

(b) _____

_____

(c) _____

_____

(d) _____

_____

(e) _____

_____

Exercise 1-12

	Accounts			Accounts	Maben	Maben,		
Cash	+ Receivable	+ Equipment =		Payable	+ Capital	- Withdrawals	+ Revenues	- Expenses
(a)								
(b)								
(c)								
(d)								
(e)								
(f)								
(g)								
(h)								
(i)								
(j)								

Exercise 1-14

Exercise 1-16

Name _____

(1) _____   (5) _____

(2) _____   (6) _____

(3) _____   (7) _____

(4) _____   (8) _____

Exercise 1-18

Return on Assets: _____

_____

_____

_____

_____

_____

Exercise 1-19

(a) _____

(b) _____

(c) _____

(d) _____

(e) _____

Chapter 1   Problem 1-1A or 1-1B   *Name* _____

Part 1: Company_____

(a) _____
_____
_____
_____
_____

(b) _____
_____
_____
_____
_____
_____
_____

(c) _____
_____
_____
_____
_____

Part 2: Company_____

(a) _____
_____
_____

(b) _____
_____
_____

(c) _____
_____
_____
_____
_____

Part 3: Company_____

_____

_____

_____

_____

_____

_____

_____

_____

_____

_____

_____

_____

_____

_____

_____

_____

_____

_____

_____

_____

Part 4: Company_____

_____
_____
_____
_____
_____
_____
_____
_____
_____
_____
_____
_____
_____
_____
_____

Part 5: Company_____

_____
_____
_____
_____
_____
_____
_____
_____
_____
_____
_____
_____
_____
_____
_____

		Balance Sheet		INCOME STMT.	Statement of Cash Flows		
TRANSACTION	TOTAL ASSETS	TOTAL LIABILITIES	TOTAL EQUITY	NET INCOME	OPERATING ACTIVITIES	FINANCING ACTIVITIES	INVESTING ACTIVITIES
1.							
2.							
3.							
4.							
5.							
6.							
7.							
8.							
9.							
10.							

_____
_____

Income Statement
For Year Ended December 31, 2005
_____
_____
_____
_____
_____
_____
_____

Problem 1-4A or 1-4B

_____

Balance Sheet
December 31, 2005
_____
_____
_____
_____
_____
_____
_____
_____
_____

Problem 1-5A or 1-5B

_____

Statement of Cash Flows
For Year Ended December 31, 2005
_____
_____
_____
_____
_____
_____
_____

Statement of Owner's Equity
For Year Ended December 31, 2005

Chapter 1   Problem 1-7A or 1-7B
Parts 1 and 2

DATE	ASSETS			=	LIABILITIES +	EQUITY			
	CASH +	ACCOUNTS RECEIVABLE +	OFFICE EQUIPMENT	=	ACCOUNTS PAYABLE +	CAPITAL −	WITHDRAWALS +	REVENUES −	EXPENSES

Income Statement

Statement of Owner's Equity

Balance Sheet

Statement of Cash Flows

Name _____

DATE	ASSETS				=	LIABILITIES	+	EQUITY			
	CASH	+ ACCOUNTS RECEIVABLE	+ OFFICE SUPPLIES	+ OFFICE EQUIPMENT	=	ACCOUNTS PAYABLE	+	CAPITAL	- WITHDRAWALS	+ REVENUES	- EXPENSES

Income Statement

Statement of Owner's Equity

Balance Sheet

Part 3

_____

_____

Statement of Cash Flows

_____

_____

_____

_____

_____

_____

_____

_____

_____

_____

_____

_____

_____

_____

_____

_____

_____

_____

Part 4

_____

_____

_____

_____

_____

_____

_____

_____

Name _____

	ASSETS					=	LIABILITIES		+	EQUITY				
	CASH	+	ACCOUNTS RECEIVABLE	+	OFFICE SUPPLIES	+	OFFICE EQUIPMENT	+	BUILDING	=	ACCOUNTS PAYABLE	+	NOTES PAYABLE	+	CAPITAL	-	WITHDRAWALS	+	REVENUES	-	EXPENSES
a.															
b.															
Bal.															
c.															
Bal.															
d.															
Bal.															
e.															
Bal.															
f.															
Bal.															
g.															
Bal.															
h.															
Bal.															
i.															
Bal.															
j.															
Bal.															
k.															
Bal.															

_____

_____

_____

(1a) _____

_____

(1b) _____

_____

(2) _____

_____

_____

(3) _____

_____

_____

(4) _____

_____

_____

_____

_____

_____

_____

(1) _____
_____
_____

(2) _____
_____
_____

(3) _____
_____
_____

(4) _____
_____
_____

Problem 1-12A or 1-12B

(1) Return: _____
_____

  Risk: _____
_____

(2) Return: _____
_____

  Risk: _____
_____

(3) Return: _____
_____

  Risk: _____
_____

(4) Return: _____
_____

  Risk: _____
_____

Chapter 1   Problem 1-13A or 1-13B   Name _____

(1) _____   (5) _____
(2) _____   (6) _____
(3) _____   (7) _____
(4) _____   (8) _____

Problem 1-14A

(1) Major Activity: _____

_____

_____

(2) Major Activity: _____

_____

_____

(3) Major Activity: _____

_____

_____

_____

Problem 1-14B

I: _____

  A. _____

  B. _____

II. _____

  A. _____

  B. _____

III. _____

  A. _____

  B. _____

_____

Chapter 1   Serial Problem   Success Systems   Name _____

| DATE | | ASSETS | | | | LIABILITIES | | EQUITY | | | |
	CASH	+ ACCOUNTS RECEIVABLE	+ COMPUTER SUPPLIES	+ OFFICE EQUIPMENT	=	ACCOUNTS PAYABLE	+ K. BREEZE, CAPITAL	K. BREEZE, - WITHDRAWALS	+ REVENUES	- EXPENSES
Oct. 1										
3										
Bal.										
6										
Bal.										
8										
Bal.										
12										
Bal.										
15										
Bal.										
17										
Bal.										
20										
Bal.										
22										
Bal.										
28										
Bal.										
31										
Bal.										
31										
Bal.										

Name _____

(1) _____
_____
_____
_____

(2) _____
_____
_____
_____
_____

(3) _____
_____
_____
_____

(4) _____
_____
_____
_____

(5) **Roll On:** _____
_____
_____
_____

Krispy Kreme	Tastykake
(1)	

(2)

(3)

(4)

(5)

Ethics Challenge--BTN 1-3

(1)

(2)

(3)

(4)

(1) --*Request For Information*--

(2)

1. _____
_____
_____
_____
_____

2. _____
_____
_____
_____

Teamwork in Action--BTN 1-6

(1) **Meeting Time and Place:**   _____
_____

(2) **Telephone and E-mail Addresses:**   _____
_____
_____
_____
_____
_____

Instructor Notification: ☐ **YES** _____

(1) _____
    1 _____
    2 _____
    3 _____
    4 _____
    5 _____
    6 _____
    7 _____
    8 _____
    9 _____
    10 _____

(2) _____
_____
_____
_____
_____

(3) _____
_____
_____
_____
_____

Entrepreneurial Decision--BTN 1-8
(1)(a) _____
_____
_____
_____
_____

  (b) _____
_____
_____
_____

(2) _____
_____
_____
_____
_____
_____
_____

(1) _____
_____
_____
_____
_____

(2) _____
_____
_____
_____
_____

(3) _____
_____
_____
_____
_____

Global Decision--BTN 1-10

(1) _____
_____
_____
_____
_____

(2) _____
_____
_____
_____
_____

Likely source documents are: _____
_____
_____
_____
_____

Quick Study 2-2

(a) _____   (f) _____
(b) _____   (g) _____
(c) _____   (h) _____
(d) _____   (i) _____
(e) _____

Quick Study 2-3

(a) _____   (g) _____
(b) _____   (h) _____
(c) _____   (i) _____
(d) _____   (j) _____
(e) _____   (k) _____
(f) _____   (l) _____

Quick Study 2-4

(a) _____   (f) _____
(b) _____   (g) _____
(c) _____   (h) _____
(d) _____   (i) _____
(e) _____   (j) _____

Quick Study 2-5

(a) _____   (e) _____
(b) _____   (f) _____
(c) _____   (g) _____
(d) _____   (h) _____

GENERAL JOURNAL

Date	Account Titles and Explanation	P.R.	Debit	Credit

Quick Study 2-7

_____

_____

_____

_____

_____

Quick Study 2-8

(a) _____   (f) _____

(b) _____   (g) _____

(c) _____   (h) _____

(d) _____   (i) _____

(e) _____   (j) _____

ACCOUNT	TYPE OF ACCOUNT	INCREASE (Dr. or Cr.)	NORMAL BALANCE
a.			
b.			
c.			
d.			
e.			
f.			
g.			
h.			
i.			
j.			
k.			
l.			

Exercise 2-2

_____

_____

_____

_____

_____

_____

_____

_____

_____

_____

_____

_____

_____

_____

_____

_____

_____

_____

(a) _____

_____

_____

_____

_____

_____

_____

(b) _____

_____

_____

_____

_____

_____

_____

(c) _____

_____

_____

_____

_____

_____

_____

GENERAL JOURNAL

Date	Account Titles and Explanation	P.R.	Debit	Credit

40

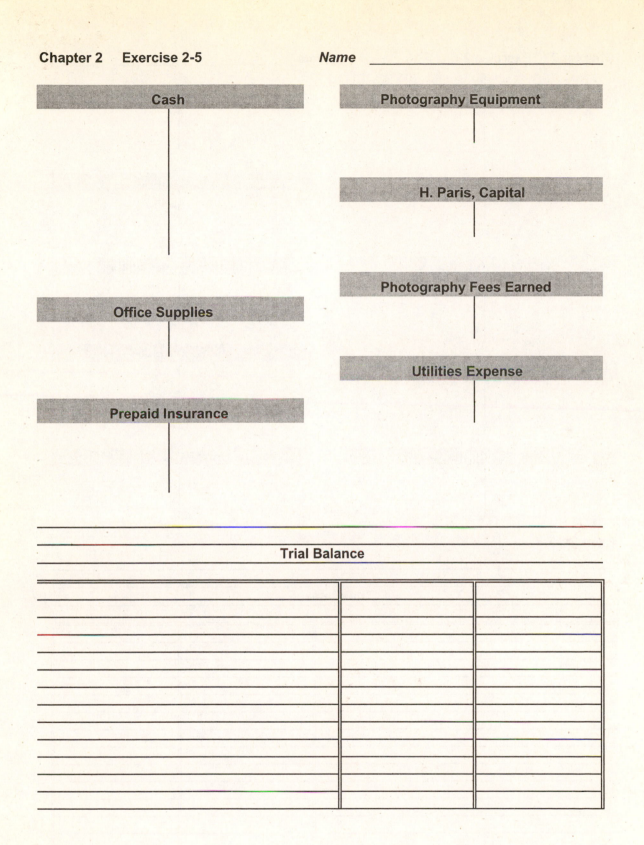

Cash		Photography Equipment	

Office Supplies		Photography Fees Earned	

Prepaid Insurance		Utilities Expense	

H. Paris, Capital	

Trial Balance

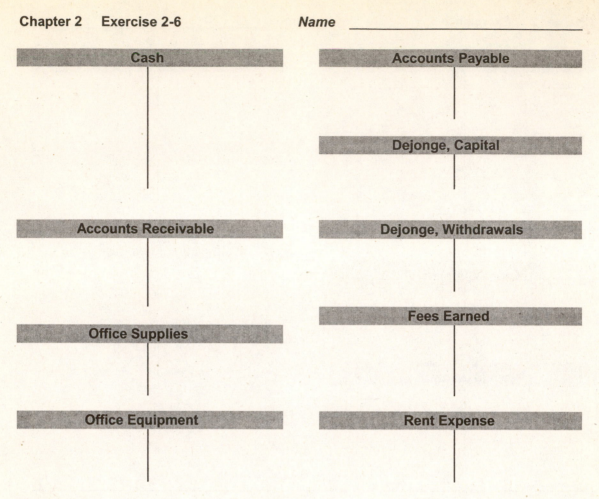

Cash

Accounts Payable

Dejonge, Capital

Accounts Receivable

Dejonge, Withdrawals

Office Supplies

Fees Earned

Office Equipment

Rent Expense

Exercise 2-7

Trial Balance		

Name _____

GENERAL JOURNAL

Date	Account Titles and Explanation	P.R.	Debit	Credit

Transactions not creating revenues and the reasons: _____

_____

_____

_____

_____

_____

_____

_____

_____

_____

_____

_____

_____

_____

_____

_____

_____

Name _____

GENERAL JOURNAL

Date		Account Titles and Explanation	P.R.	Debit	Credit

Transactions not creating revenues and the reasons: _____

_____

_____

_____

_____

_____

_____

_____

_____

_____

_____

_____

_____

_____

_____

_____

Name _____

Income Statement

_____
_____
_____
_____
_____
_____
_____
_____
_____
_____
_____
_____
_____
_____
_____

Exercise 2-11

Statement of Owner's Equity

_____
_____
_____
_____
_____
_____
_____
_____
_____
_____
_____
_____

_____

Balance Sheet

_____

(a) Net Income (Loss) = ⬚

     Supporting Computations: _____

_____

_____

_____

_____

_____

_____

_____

_____

(b) Net Income (Loss) = ⬚

     Supporting Computations: _____

_____

_____

_____

_____

_____

_____

_____

_____

(c) Net Income (Loss) = ⬚

     Supporting Computations: _____

_____

_____

_____

_____

_____

_____

_____

_____

(d) Net Income (Loss) = ⬚

     Supporting Computations: _____

_____

_____

_____

_____

_____

_____

_____

Name _____

	(a)	(b)	(c)	(d)

Exercise 2-15

(a) _____

(b) _____

(c) _____

(d) _____

(e) _____

(f) _____

(g) _____

_____

Name _____

GENERAL JOURNAL

	Date	Account Titles and Explanation	P.R.	Debit	Credit
(a)					
(b)					
(c)					
(d)					
(e)					
(f)					
(g)					

	Description	(1) Difference between Debit and Credit Columns	(2) Column with the Larger Total	(3) Identify account(s) incorrectly stated	(4) Amount that account(s) is overstate or understated
(a)	$2,400 debit to Rent Expense is posted as a $1,590 debit.	$810	Credit	Rent Expense	Rent Expense is understated by $810
(b)					
(c)					
(d)					
(e)					
(f)					
(g)					

(a) _____

_____

_____

(b) _____

_____

_____

(c) _____

_____

_____

(d) _____

_____

_____

(e) _____

_____

_____

_____

Part a

(1) _____

_____

(2) _____

_____

(3) _____

_____

(4) _____

_____

(5) _____

_____

(6) _____

_____

Part b

_____

_____

_____

_____

Part c

_____

_____

_____

_____

Part d

_____

_____

_____

_____

Part e

_____

_____

Part f

_____

_____

_____

Name _____

GENERAL JOURNAL

Date		Account Titles and Explanation	P.R.	Debit	Credit

Date	Account Titles and Explanation	P.R.	Debit	Credit

GENERAL LEDGER

Cash   ACCOUNT NO. 101

Date	Explanation	P.R.	DEBIT	CREDIT	BALANCE

Accounts Receivable   ACCOUNT NO. 106

Date	Explanation	P.R.	DEBIT	CREDIT	BALANCE

Office Supplies   ACCOUNT NO. 124

Date	Explanation	P.R.	DEBIT	CREDIT	BALANCE

Prepaid Insurance   ACCOUNT NO. 128

Date	Explanation	P.R.	DEBIT	CREDIT	BALANCE

Prepaid Rent   ACCOUNT NO. 131

Date	Explanation	P.R.	DEBIT	CREDIT	BALANCE

Office Equipment   ACCOUNT NO. 163

Date	Explanation	P.R.	DEBIT	CREDIT	BALANCE

Accounts Payable   ACCOUNT NO. 201

Date	Explanation	P.R.	DEBIT	CREDIT	BALANCE

_____,Capital   ACCOUNT NO. 301

Date	Explanation	P.R.	DEBIT	CREDIT	BALANCE

_____, Withdrawals   ACCOUNT NO. 302

Date	Explanation	P.R.	DEBIT	CREDIT	BALANCE

Date	Explanation	P.R.	DEBIT	CREDIT	BALANCE

Service Fees Earned**   ACCOUNT NO. 401

Date	Explanation	P.R.	DEBIT	CREDIT	BALANCE

Services Revenue*   ACCOUNT NO. 403

Date	Explanation	P.R.	DEBIT	CREDIT	BALANCE

Utilities Expense   ACCOUNT NO. 690

* Problem 2-1A only.
** Problem 2-1B only

Trial Balance

GENERAL JOURNAL

Date	Account Titles and Explanation	P.R.	Debit	Credit

GENERAL JOURNAL

Date	Account Titles and Explanation	P.R.	Debit	Credit

Cash   No. 101

DATE	PR	Debit	Credit	Balance

Accounts Payable   No. 201

DATE	PR	Debit	Credit	Balance

Notes Payable   No. 250

DATE	PR	Debit	Credit	Balance

_____,Capital   No. 301

DATE	PR	Debit	Credit	Balance

Accounts Receivable   No. 106

DATE	PR	Debit	Credit	Balance

_____,Withdrawals   No. 302

DATE	PR	Debit	Credit	Balance

Prepaid Insurance   No. 108

DATE	PR	Debit	Credit	Balance

_____Fees Earned   No. 402

DATE	PR	Debit	Credit	Balance

Office Equipment   No. 163

DATE	PR	Debit	Credit	Balance

Wages Expense   No. 601

DATE	PR	Debit	Credit	Balance

_____Equipment   No. 164

DATE	PR	Debit	Credit	Balance

_____Rental Expense   No. 602

DATE	PR	Debit	Credit	Balance

Building   No. 170

DATE	PR	Debit	Credit	Balance

Advertising Expense   No. 603

DATE	PR	Debit	Credit	Balance

Land   No. 172

DATE	PR	Debit	Credit	Balance

Repairs Expense   No. 604

DATE	PR	Debit	Credit	Balance

Chapter 2   Problem 2-2A or 2-2B   Name _____
Part 3

Trial Balance

GENERAL JOURNAL

Date	Account Titles and Explanation	P.R.	Debit	Credit

Date		Account Titles and Explanation	P.R.	Debit	Credit

GENERAL LEDGER

Cash   ACCOUNT NO. 101

Date	Explanation	P.R.	DEBIT	CREDIT	BALANCE

Accounts Receivable   ACCOUNT NO. 106

Date	Explanation	P.R.	DEBIT	CREDIT	BALANCE

Office Supplies   ACCOUNT NO. 124

Date	Explanation	P.R.	DEBIT	CREDIT	BALANCE

Prepaid Insurance   ACCOUNT NO. 128

Date	Explanation	P.R.	DEBIT	CREDIT	BALANCE

Prepaid Rent   **ACCOUNT NO. 131**

Date	Explanation	P.R.	DEBIT	CREDIT	BALANCE

Office Equipment   **ACCOUNT NO. 163**

Date	Explanation	P.R.	DEBIT	CREDIT	BALANCE

Accounts Payable   **ACCOUNT NO. 201**

Date	Explanation	P.R.	DEBIT	CREDIT	BALANCE

_____ ,Capital   **ACCOUNT NO. 301**

Date	Explanation	P.R.	DEBIT	CREDIT	BALANCE

_____ , Withdrawals   **ACCOUNT NO. 302**

Date	Explanation	P.R.	DEBIT	CREDIT	BALANCE

Services Revenue   ACCOUNT NO. 403

Date	Explanation	P.R.	DEBIT	CREDIT	BALANCE

Utilities Expense   ACCOUNT NO. 690

Date	Explanation	P.R.	DEBIT	CREDIT	BALANCE

Part 3

Trial Balance

Name _____

_____
_____
Balance Sheet
_____
_____
_____
_____
_____
_____
_____
_____
_____
_____
_____
_____
_____
_____

Balance Sheet
_____
_____
_____
_____
_____
_____
_____
_____
_____
_____
_____
_____
_____
_____

Part 2

Net Income Computation: _____

_____
_____
_____
_____
_____
_____
_____
_____
_____
_____
_____

Part 3

Debt Ratio: _____

_____
_____
_____
_____
_____

Part 1

Trial Balance

Part 2

Seven Most Likely Transactions (following order of trial balance):

(1) _____

(2) _____

(3) _____

(4) _____

(5) _____

(6) _____

(7) _____

Report of Cash Received and Cash Paid

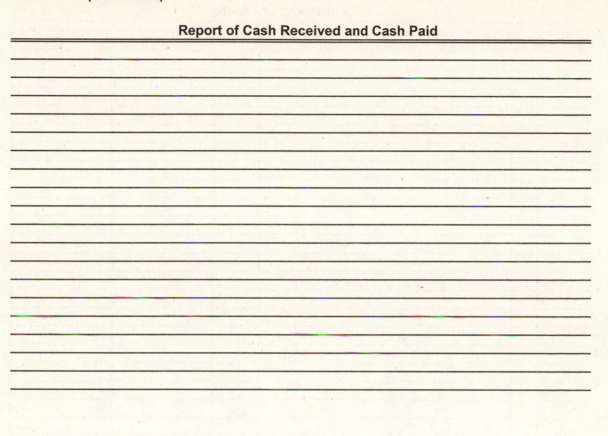

GENERAL JOURNAL

Date		Account Titles and Explanation	P.R.	Debit	Credit

Date		Account Titles and Explanation	P.R.	Debit	Credit

Part 2

Cash   No. 101

DATE	PR	Debit	Credit	Balance

Land   No. 172

DATE	PR	Debit	Credit	Balance

Accounts Payable   No. 201

DATE	PR	Debit	Credit	Balance

Notes Payable   No. 250

DATE	PR	Debit	Credit	Balance

Accounts Receivable   No. 106

DATE	PR	Debit	Credit	Balance

_____,Capital   No. 301

DATE	PR	Debit	Credit	Balance

Office Supplies   No. 108

DATE	PR	Debit	Credit	Balance

_____,Withdrawals   No. 302

DATE	PR	Debit	Credit	Balance

Office Equipment   No. 163

DATE	PR	Debit	Credit	Balance

Fees Earned   No. 402

DATE	PR	Debit	Credit	Balance

Automobiles   No. 164

DATE	PR	Debit	Credit	Balance

Salaries Expense   No. 601

DATE	PR	Debit	Credit	Balance

Building   No. 170

DATE	PR	Debit	Credit	Balance

Utilities Expense   No. 602

DATE	PR	Debit	Credit	Balance

_____

Trial Balance

GENERAL JOURNAL

Date	Account Titles and Explanation	P.R.	Debit	Credit

Date	Account Titles and Explanation	P.R.	Debit	Credit

Date	Account Titles and Explanation	P.R.	Debit	Credit

Name _____

GENERAL LEDGER

Cash   ACCOUNT NO. 101

Date	Explanation	P.R.	DEBIT	CREDIT	BALANCE

Accounts Receivable   ACCOUNT NO. 106

Date	Explanation	P.R.	DEBIT	CREDIT	BALANCE

Computer Supplies   ACCOUNT NO. 126

Date	Explanation	P.R.	DEBIT	CREDIT	BALANCE

Prepaid Insurance   ACCOUNT NO. 128

Date	Explanation	P.R.	DEBIT	CREDIT	BALANCE

Prepaid Rent   ACCOUNT NO. 131

Date	Explanation	P.R.	DEBIT	CREDIT	BALANCE

Office Equipment   ACCOUNT NO. 163

Date	Explanation	P.R.	DEBIT	CREDIT	BALANCE

Computer Equipment   ACCOUNT NO. 167

Date	Explanation	P.R.	DEBIT	CREDIT	BALANCE

Accounts Payable   ACCOUNT NO. 201

Date	Explanation	P.R.	DEBIT	CREDIT	BALANCE

K. Breeze, Capital   ACCOUNT NO. 301

Date	Explanation	P.R.	DEBIT	CREDIT	BALANCE

K. Breeze, Withdrawals   ACCOUNT NO. 302

Date	Explanation	P.R.	DEBIT	CREDIT	BALANCE

Computer Services Revenue   ACCOUNT NO. 403

Date	Explanation	P.R.	DEBIT	CREDIT	BALANCE

Wages Expense   ACCOUNT NO. 623

Date	Explanation	P.R.	DEBIT	CREDIT	BALANCE

Advertising Expense   ACCOUNT NO. 655

Date	Explanation	P.R.	DEBIT	CREDIT	BALANCE

Mileage Expense   ACCOUNT NO. 676

Date	Explanation	P.R.	DEBIT	CREDIT	BALANCE

Miscellaneous Expense   ACCOUNT NO. 677

Date	Explanation	P.R.	DEBIT	CREDIT	BALANCE

Repairs Expense-Computer   ACCOUNT NO. 684

Date	Explanation	P.R.	DEBIT	CREDIT	BALANCE

Name _____

Trial Balance

(1) _____
_____
_____

(2) _____
_____
_____

(3) _____
_____
_____
_____

(4) _____
_____
_____

(5) Roll On: _____
_____
_____
_____
_____
_____

Comparative Analysis--BTN 2-2

(1) Current Year Debt Ratio _____
_____

Prior Year Debt Ratio _____
_____

(2) Current Year Debt Ratio _____
_____

Prior Year Debt Ratio _____
_____

(3) _____
_____
_____
_____
_____
_____

_____
_____
_____
_____
_____
_____
_____
_____
_____
_____
_____
_____
_____
_____
_____
_____

MEMORANDUM

TO:

FROM:

SUBJECT:

DATE:

_____

_____

_____

_____

_____

_____

_____

_____

_____

_____

_____

_____

_____

_____

_____

_____

_____

_____

_____

_____

_____

_____

_____

_____

_____

_____

_____

_____

_____

_____

_____

_____

_____

_____

_____

_____

_____

(1) _____

_____

_____

_____

_____

_____

(2) _____

_____

_____

_____

_____

_____

(3) _____

_____

_____

_____

_____

_____

_____

Name _____

(1) Component selected: _____
_____

(2) (a) _____
_____

   (b) _____
_____

   (c) _____
_____

   (d) _____
_____

   (e) _____
_____
_____

(3) Presentation Notes: _____
_____
_____
_____
_____
_____
_____

Business Week Activity--BTN 2-7

(1) _____
_____
_____
_____

(2) _____
_____

(3) _____
_____
_____
_____
_____

(1) _____

Balance Sheet

(2) _____

(3) _____

(1) _____
_____
_____
_____
_____
_____

(2) _____
_____
_____
_____
_____
_____

(1) _____

_____

_____

_____

_____

_____

(2) _____

_____

_____

_____

_____

_____

_____

(3) _____

_____

_____

_____

_____

(4) _____

_____

_____

_____

_____

_____

(1) _____

_____

_____

(2) _____

_____

_____

(3) _____

_____

_____

(a) _____

(b) _____

(c) _____

(d) _____

(e) _____

Quick Study 3-2

GENERAL JOURNAL

	Date		Account Titles and Explanation	P.R	Debit	Credit
(a)						
(b)						

Quick Study 3-3

GENERAL JOURNAL

	Date		Account Titles and Explanation	P.R	Debit	Credit
(a)						

(b) _____

_____

_____

_____

GENERAL JOURNAL

Date		Account Titles and Explanation	P.R	Debit	Credit
(a)					
(b)					

Quick Study 3-5

GENERAL JOURNAL

Date		Account Titles and Explanation	P.R	Debit	Credit

Quick Study 3-6

	Dr./Cr.	Account Titles	Financial Statement
(a)	Debit		
	Credit		
(b)	Debit		
	Credit		
(c)	Debit		
	Credit		
(d)	Debit		
	Credit		
(e)	Debit		
	Credit		

Name _____

Debit	Credit
(1)	
(2)	
(3)	

Quick Study 3-8

Answer is _____

Supporting work: _____
_____
_____
_____
_____
_____

Quick Study 3-9

Cash Basis: _____
_____
_____
_____
_____
_____

Accrual Basis _____
_____
_____
_____
_____
_____

Quick Study 3-10

Answer is _____

Supporting work: _____
_____
_____
_____
_____

Profit Margin: _____

_____

_____

_____

_____

_____

Interpretation of Profit Margin: _____

_____

_____

_____

_____

_____

Quick Study 3-12

Answer is _____

Supporting work: _____

_____

_____

_____

Exercise 3-1

(1) _____	(4) _____
(2) _____	(5) _____
(3) _____	(6) _____

GENERAL JOURNAL

Date	Account Titles and Explanation	P.R	Debit	Credit
(a)				
(b)				
(c)				
(d)				
(e)				
(f)				
(g)				

Notes: _____

_____

_____

_____

_____

GENERAL JOURNAL

Date	Account Titles and Explanation	P.R	Debit	Credit
(a)				
(b)				
(c)				
(d)				
(e)				
(f)				

Notes: _____
_____
_____
_____

Name _____

GENERAL JOURNAL

Date		Account Titles and Explanation	P.R	Debit	Credit
Adjusting Entry:					
Payday Entry:					

Exercise 3-5

(a) _____

_____

_____

(b) _____

_____

_____

(c) _____

_____

_____

(d) _____

_____

_____

(a)

GENERAL JOURNAL

Date	Account Titles and Explanation	P.R.	Debit	Credit
Adjusting Entry:				
Journal Entry (Next Period):				

(b)

GENERAL JOURNAL

Date	Account Titles and Explanation	P.R	Debit	Credit
Adjusting Entry:				
Journal Entry (Next Period):				

(c)

GENERAL JOURNAL

Date	Account Titles and Explanation	P.R.	Debit	Credit
Adjusting Entry:				
Journal Entry (Next Period):				

Exercise 3-7

	Balance Sheet Insurance Asset Using:			Insurance Expense Using:	
Date of:	*Accrual Basis*	*Cash Basis*	*Year*	*Accrual Basis*	*Cash Basis*
12/31/2003			2003		
12/31/2004			2004		
12/31/2005			2005		
12/31/2006			2006		
			Total		

Supporting work:

GENERAL JOURNAL

Date		Account Titles and Explanation	P.R.	Debit	Credit

Profit Margin Calculation:

(a) _____

_____

(b) _____

_____

(c) _____

_____

(d) _____

_____

(e) _____

_____

Most Profitable: _____

Interpretation of Profit Margin: _____

_____

_____

GENERAL JOURNAL

Date	Account Titles and Explanation	P.R.	Debit	Credit
(a)				
(b)				
(c)				
(d)				
(e)				
(f)				
(g)				

Name _____

GENERAL JOURNAL

Date	Account Titles and Explanation	P.R.	Debit	Credit
(a)				
(b)				

(c)
Method in Part (a):
      Unearned Fees = $ _____

      Fees Earned   = $ _____

Method in Part (b):
      Unearned Fees = $ _____

      Fees Earned   = $ _____

(1)	_____	(7)	_____
(2)	_____	(8)	_____
(3)	_____	(9)	_____
(4)	_____	(10)	_____
(5)	_____	(11)	_____
(6)	_____	(12)	_____

Problem 3-2A or 3-2B
Part 1   GENERAL JOURNAL

Date	Account Titles and Explanation	P.R.	Debit	Credit

GENERAL JOURNAL

Date	Account Titles and Explanation	P.R.	Debit	Credit

Name _____

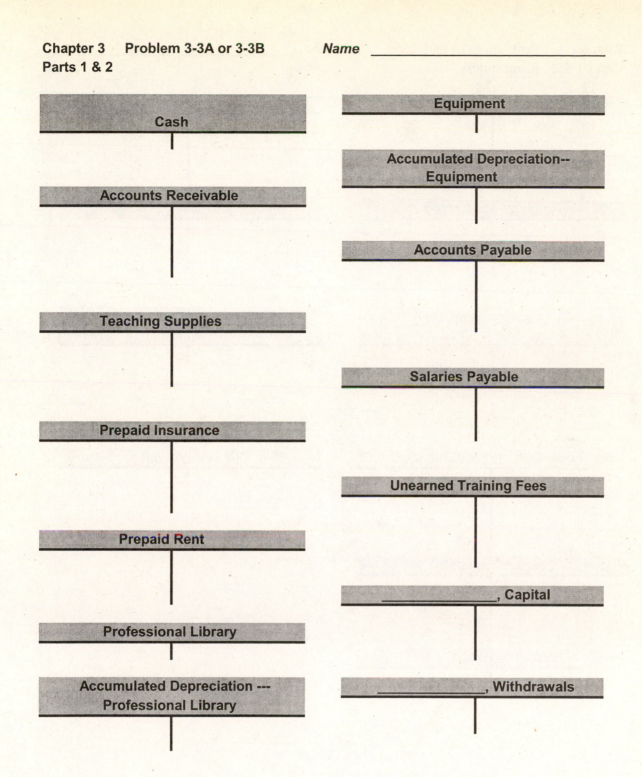

Cash

Accounts Receivable

Teaching Supplies

Prepaid Insurance

Prepaid Rent

Professional Library

**Accumulated Depreciation ---
Professional Library**

Equipment

**Accumulated Depreciation--
Equipment**

Accounts Payable

Salaries Payable

Unearned Training Fees

_____, Capital

_____, Withdrawals

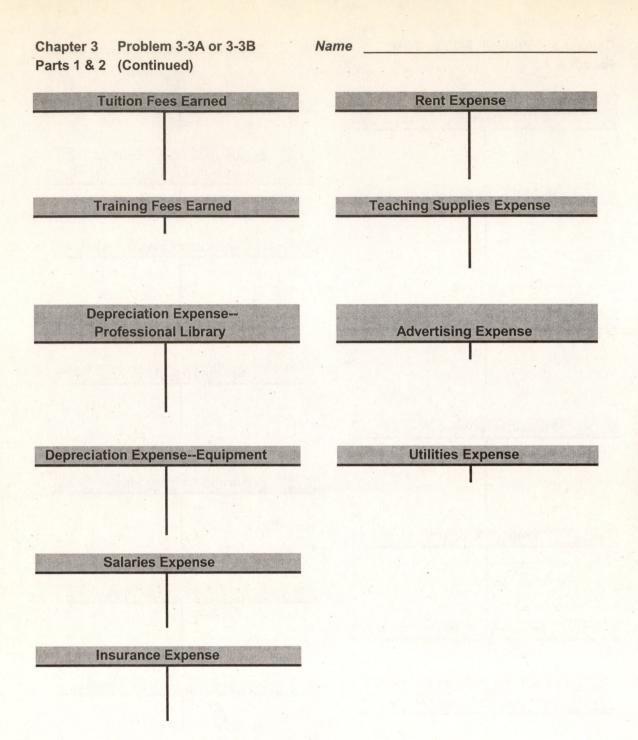

Tuition Fees Earned

Training Fees Earned

**Depreciation Expense--
Professional Library**

Depreciation Expense--Equipment

Salaries Expense

Insurance Expense

Rent Expense

Teaching Supplies Expense

Advertising Expense

Utilities Expense

GENERAL JOURNAL

Date	Account Titles and Explanation	P.R.	Debit	Credit

Adjusted Trial Balance

Income Statement

Statement of Owner's Equity

Balance Sheet

ACCOUNT TITLES	UNADJUSTED TRIAL BALANCE		ADJUSTMENTS		ADJUSTED TRIAL BALANCE	
	DR	CR	DR	CR	DR	CR

Adjustment Descriptions

(a) _____

(b) _____

(c) _____

(d) _____

(e) _____

(f) _____

(g) _____

(h) _____

Income Statement

Statement of Owner's Equity

Balance Sheet

Income Statement

Statement of Owner's Equity

_____

_____

Balance Sheet

_____

_____

_____

_____

_____

_____

_____

_____

_____

_____

_____

_____

_____

_____

_____

_____

_____

_____

_____

_____

_____

_____

_____

_____

Part 2

Profit Margin:

GENERAL JOURNAL

Date		Account Titles and Explanation	P.R.	Debit	Credit

GENERAL JOURNAL

Date		Account Titles and Explanation	P.R.	Debit	Credit

_____
_____
_____
_____
_____
_____
_____
_____
_____
_____
_____
_____
_____
_____
_____
_____
_____
_____
_____
_____
_____
_____

GENERAL JOURNAL

Date	Account Titles and Explanation	P.R.	Debit	Credit

Name _____

GENERAL JOURNAL

Date	Account Titles and Explanation	P.R.	Debit	Credit

Name _____

GENERAL LEDGER

Cash — ACCOUNT NO. 101

Date	Explanation	P.R.	DEBIT	CREDIT	BALANCE
2004 Nov. 30	Balance				48,052

Accounts Receivable — ACCOUNT NO. 106

Date	Explanation	P.R.	DEBIT	CREDIT	BALANCE
2004 Nov. 30	Balance				12,618

Computer Supplies — ACCOUNT NO. 126

Date	Explanation	P.R.	DEBIT	CREDIT	BALANCE
2004 Nov. 30	Balance				2,545

	Prepaid Insurance				ACCOUNT NO. 128
Date	Explanation	P.R.	DEBIT	CREDIT	BALANCE
2004 Nov. 30	Balance				2,220

	Prepaid Rent				ACCOUNT NO. 131
Date	Explanation	P.R.	DEBIT	CREDIT	BALANCE
2004 Nov. 30	Balance				3,300

	Office Equipment				ACCOUNT NO. 163
Date	Explanation	P.R.	DEBIT	CREDIT	BALANCE
2004 Nov. 30	Balance				8,000

	Accumulated Depreciation--Office Equipment				ACCOUNT NO. 164
Date	Explanation	P.R.	DEBIT	CREDIT	BALANCE

	Computer Equipment				ACCOUNT NO. 167
Date	Explanation	P.R.	DEBIT	CREDIT	BALANCE
2004 Nov. 30	Balance				20,000

Name _____

Accumulated Depreciation--Computer Equipment ACCOUNT NO. 168

Date	Explanation	P.R.	DEBIT	CREDIT	BALANCE

Accounts Payable ACCOUNT NO. 201

Date	Explanation	P.R.	DEBIT	CREDIT	BALANCE
2004 Nov. 30	Balance				0

Wages Payable ACCOUNT NO. 210

Date	Explanation	P.R.	DEBIT	CREDIT	BALANCE

Unearned Computer Services Revenue ACCOUNT NO. 236

Date	Explanation	P.R.	DEBIT	CREDIT	BALANCE

K. Breeze, Capital ACCOUNT NO. 301

Date	Explanation	P.R.	DEBIT	CREDIT	BALANCE
2004 Nov. 30	Balance				83,000

Name _____

K. Breeze, Withdrawals   ACCOUNT NO. 302

Date	Explanation	P.R.	DEBIT	CREDIT	BALANCE
2004 Nov. 30	Balance				5,600

Computer Services Revenue   ACCOUNT NO. 403

Date	Explanation	P.R.	DEBIT	CREDIT	BALANCE
2004 Nov. 30	Balance				25,659

Depreciation Expense--Office Equipment   ACCOUNT NO. 612

Date	Explanation	P.R.	DEBIT	CREDIT	BALANCE

Depreciation Expense--Computer Equipment   ACCOUNT NO. 613

Date	Explanation	P.R.	DEBIT	CREDIT	BALANCE

Wages Expense   ACCOUNT NO. 623

Date	Explanation	P.R.	DEBIT	CREDIT	BALANCE
2004 Nov. 30	Balance				2,625

Insurance Expense   ACCOUNT NO. 637

Date	Explanation	P.R.	DEBIT	CREDIT	BALANCE

Rent Expense   ACCOUNT NO. 640

Date	Explanation	P.R.	DEBIT	CREDIT	BALANCE

Computer Supplies Expense   ACCOUNT NO. 652

Date	Explanation	P.R.	DEBIT	CREDIT	BALANCE

Advertising Expense   ACCOUNT NO. 655

Date	Explanation	P.R.	DEBIT	CREDIT	BALANCE
2004 Nov. 30	Balance				1,940

Mileage Expense   ACCOUNT NO. 676

Date	Explanation	P.R.	DEBIT	CREDIT	BALANCE
2004 Nov. 30	Balance				704

Miscellaneous Expense   ACCOUNT NO. 677

Date	Explanation	P.R.	DEBIT	CREDIT	BALANCE
2004 Nov. 30	Balance				250

Repairs Expense--Computer   ACCOUNT NO. 684

Date	Explanation	P.R.	DEBIT	CREDIT	BALANCE
2004 Nov. 30	Balance				805

Income Summary   ACCOUNT NO. 901

Date	Explanation	P.R.	DEBIT	CREDIT	BALANCE

Name _____

SUCCESS SYSTEMS
Adjusted Trial Balance
December 31, 2004

SUCCESS SYSTEMS

Income Statement

For Three Months Ended December 31, 2004

Part 5

SUCCESS SYSTEMS

Statement of Owner's Equity

For Three Months Ended December 31, 2004

SUCCESS SYSTEMS
Balance Sheet
December 31, 2004

(1) _____

_____

_____

(2) _____

_____

_____

_____

_____

_____

_____

_____

_____

_____

_____

_____

_____

_____

(3) 2003 Profit Margin: _____

_____

_____

2002 Profit Margin: _____

_____

_____

(4) Roll On: _____

_____

_____

_____

_____

_____

(1) Krispy Kreme

    Current Year Profit Margin:

    Prior Year Profit Margin:

    Tastykake

    Current Year Profit Margin:

    Prior Year Profit Margin:

(2) Analysis

(1) _____

_____

_____

_____

_____

_____

_____

_____

(2) _____

_____

_____

_____

_____

_____

_____

_____

_____

_____

(3) _____

_____

_____

_____

_____

_____

_____

_____

_____

MEMORANDUM

TO:

FROM:

SUBJECT:

DATE:

(1) _____

_____

_____

_____

_____

(2) _____

(3) _____

_____

_____

_____

(4) _____

_____

_____

_____

(5) _____

_____

_____

_____

(6) _____

_____

_____

_____

(7) _____

_____

_____

_____

_____

(1) _____
_____
_____
_____
_____
_____

(2) _____
_____
_____
_____
_____
_____
_____

(3) _____
_____
_____
_____
_____

(4) _____
_____
_____
_____
_____

Name _____

(1) _____
_____
_____
_____
_____
_____

(2) _____
_____
_____
_____

(3) _____
_____
_____

(4) _____
_____
_____
_____

(5) _____
_____
_____
_____

_____
_____
_____
_____
_____
_____

Global Decision--BTN 3-10

(1) _____
_____
_____
_____

(2) _____
_____
_____
_____
_____

(3) 2002 Profit Margin: _____
_____

2001 Profit Margin: _____
_____
_____
_____

_____

_____

_____

_____

_____

_____

_____

_____

_____

_____

Quick Study 4-2

Steps

1st _____

2nd _____

3rd _____

4th _____

5th _____

6th _____

7th _____

8th _____

9th _____

Quick Study 4-3

(1) _____   (5) _____

(2) _____   (6) _____

(3) _____   (7) _____

(4) _____   (8) _____

Quick Study 4-4

_____

_____

_____

_____

_____

_____

_____

_____

_____

_____

_____
_____
_____
_____
_____
_____
_____
_____
_____

Quick Study 4-6

(a) _____   (d) _____
(b) _____   (e) _____
(c) _____   (f) _____

Quick Study 4-7

(a) _____   (d) _____
(b) _____   (e) _____
(c) _____

Terrel Company
Worksheet

ACCOUNT TITLE	Unadjusted Trial Balance		Adjustments		Adjusted Trial Balance		Income Statement		Balance Sheet and Statement of Owner's Equity	
	Dr.	Cr.	Dr.	Cr.	Dr.	Cr.	Dr.	Cr.	Dr.	Cr.
Prepaid rent										
Service revenue										
Wages expense										
Accounts receivable										
Wages payable										
Rent expense										

GENERAL JOURNAL

Date	Account Titles and Explanation	P. R.	Debit	Credit

Quick Study 4-10

_____

_____

_____

_____

Quick Study 4-11[A]

GENERAL JOURNAL

Date	Account Titles and Explanation	P. R.	Debit	Credit

Name _____

GENERAL JOURNAL

Date	Account Titles and Explanation	P. R.	Debit	Credit

Posted accounts:

M.Mallon, Capital   No. 301

DATE	PR	Debit	Credit	Balance
Mar. 31				42,000

M. Mallon, Withdrawals   No. 302

DATE	PR	Debit	Credit	Balance
Mar. 31				25,000

Service Revenue   No. 401

DATE	PR	Debit	Credit	Balance
Mar. 31				74,000

Depreciation Expense   No. 603

DATE	PR	Debit	Credit	Balance
Mar. 31				17,000

Salaries Expense   No. 622

DATE	PR	Debit	Credit	Balance
Mar. 31				21,000

Insurance Expense   No. 637

DATE	PR	Debit	Credit	Balance
Mar. 31				4,500

Rent Expense   No. 640

DATE	PR	Debit	Credit	Balance
Mar. 31				9,600

Income Summary   No. 901

DATE	PR	Debit	Credit	Balance

NO.	ACCOUNT TITLE	ADJUSTED TRIAL BALANCE		AMOUNTS FOR CLOSING ENTRIES		POST-CLOSING TRIAL BALANCE	
		DR	CR	DR	CR	DR	CR

1. Closing

GENERAL JOURNAL

Date	Account Titles and Explanation	P. R.	Debit	Credit

2. Post-closing Trial Balance

Post-Closing Trial Balance

Balance Sheet

Income Statement

Statement of Owner's Equity

Name _____

Current Ratio: _____
_____
_____
_____
_____
_____
_____
_____

Interpretation: _____
_____
_____
_____
_____

Exercise 4-7

	Current Assets	Current Liabilities	Current Ratio
Case 1			
Case 2			
Case 3			
Case 4			
Case 5			

Analysis: _____
_____
_____
_____
_____

GENERAL JOURNAL

Date	Account Titles and Explanation	P. R.	Debit	Credit
(a)				
(b)				
(c)				
(d)				
(e)				

Exercise 4-9

(1)	(5)	(9)	(13)
(2)	(6)	(10)	(14)
(3)	(7)	(11)	(15)
(4)	(8)	(12)	(16)

NO.	ACCOUNT TITLE	ADJUSTED TRIAL BALANCE		INCOME STATEMENT		BALANCE SHEET & STATEMENT OF OWNER'S EQUITY	
		DR	CR	DR	CR	DR	Cr

Account Title	Debit	Credit
Rent earned		
Salaries expense		
Insurance expense		
Dock rental expense		
Boat supplies expense		
Depreciation expense--Boats		
Totals		
Net Income		
Totals		

GENERAL JOURNAL

Date	Account Titles and Explanation	P. R.	Debit	Credit

Name _____

Dalton Delivery Company
Work Sheet
For Year Ended December 31, 2005

ACCOUNT TITLE	Unadjusted Trial Balance		Adjustments		Adjusted Trial Balance		Income Statement		Balance Sheet and Statement of Owner's Equity	
	Dr.	Cr.	Dr.	Cr.	Dr.	Cr.	Dr.	Cr.	Dr.	Cr.

2. Closing Entries

GENERAL JOURNAL

Date	Account Titles and Explanation	P. R.	Debit	Credit

On the Balance Sheet: _____

_____

_____

_____

_____

_____

GENERAL JOURNAL

Date	Account Titles and Explanation	P. R.	Debit	Credit

Part 2

GENERAL JOURNAL

Date	Account Titles and Explanation	P. R.	Debit	Credit

Part 3

GENERAL JOURNAL

Date	Account Titles and Explanation	P. R.	Debit	Credit

GENERAL JOURNAL

Date	Account Titles and Explanation	P. R.	Debit	Credit

Problem 4-1A or 4-1B

(1) _____	(6) _____	(11) _____	(16) _____
(2) _____	(7) _____	(12) _____	(17) _____
(3) _____	(8) _____	(13) _____	(18) _____
(4) _____	(9) _____	(14) _____	(19) _____
(5) _____	(10) _____	(15) _____	(20) _____

GENERAL JOURNAL

Cash   ACCOUNT NO. 101

DATE	EXPLANATION	P.R.	DEBIT	CREDIT	BALANCE

Accounts Receivable   ACCOUNT NO. 106

DATE	EXPLANATION	P.R.	DEBIT	CREDIT	BALANCE

Office Supplies   ACCOUNT NO. 124

DATE	EXPLANATION	P.R.	DEBIT	CREDIT	BALANCE

Prepaid Insurance   ACCOUNT NO. 128

DATE	EXPLANATION	P.R.	DEBIT	CREDIT	BALANCE

Computer Equipment*   ACCOUNT NO. 167

DATE	EXPLANATION	P.R.	DEBIT	CREDIT	BALANCE

Accumulated Depreciation-Computer Equipment*   ACCOUNT NO. 168

DATE	EXPLANATION	P.R.	DEBIT	CREDIT	BALANCE

Building**   ACCOUNT NO. 173

DATE	EXPLANATION	P.R.	DEBIT	CREDIT	BALANCE

Accumulated Depreciation-Buildings**   ACCOUNT NO. 174

DATE	EXPLANATION	P.R.	DEBIT	CREDIT	BALANCE

Salaries Payable   ACCOUNT NO. 209

DATE	EXPLANATION	P.R.	DEBIT	CREDIT	BALANCE

_____, Capital   ACCOUNT NO. 301

DATE	EXPLANATION	P.R.	DEBIT	CREDIT	BALANCE

* Problem 4-2A only.

** Problem 4-2B only.

_____, Withdrawals   ACCOUNT NO. 302

DATE	EXPLANATION	P.R.	DEBIT	CREDIT	BALANCE

Storage Fees Earned**   ACCOUNT NO. 401

DATE	EXPLANATION	P.R.	DEBIT	CREDIT	BALANCE

Commissions Earned*   ACCOUNT NO. 405

DATE	EXPLANATION	P.R.	DEBIT	CREDIT	BALANCE

Depreciation Expense--Buildings**   ACCOUNT NO. 606

DATE	EXPLANATION	P.R.	DEBIT	CREDIT	BALANCE

Depreciation Expense-Computer Equipment*   ACCOUNT NO. 612

DATE	EXPLANATION	P.R.	DEBIT	CREDIT	BALANCE

* Problem 4-2A only.

** Problem 4-2B only.

Salaries Expense   ACCOUNT NO. 622

DATE	EXPLANATION	P.R.	DEBIT	CREDIT	BALANCE

Insurance Expense   ACCOUNT NO. 637

DATE	EXPLANATION	P.R.	DEBIT	CREDIT	BALANCE

Rent Expense   ACCOUNT NO. 640

DATE	EXPLANATION	P.R.	DEBIT	CREDIT	BALANCE

Office Supplies Expense   ACCOUNT NO. 650

DATE	EXPLANATION	P.R.	DEBIT	CREDIT	BALANCE

Repairs Expense   ACCOUNT NO. 684

DATE	EXPLANATION	P.R.	DEBIT	CREDIT	BALANCE

Telephone Expense   ACCOUNT NO. 688

DATE	EXPLANATION	P.R.	DEBIT	CREDIT	BALANCE

	Income Summary			**ACCOUNT NO. 901**	
DATE	**EXPLANATION**	**P.R.**	**DEBIT**	**CREDIT**	**BALANCE**

Name _____

GENERAL JOURNAL

Date	Account Titles and Explanation	P. R.	Debit	Credit

Unadjusted Trial Balance

GENERAL JOURNAL

Date		Account Titles and Explanation	P. R.	Debit	Credit

Income Statement

Statement of Owner's Equity

Balance Sheet

Closing Entries:

GENERAL JOURNAL

Date	Account Titles and Explanation	P. R.	Debit	Credit

Part 7

_____

Post-Closing Trial Balance

_____

Income Statement

Statement of Owner's Equity

Balance Sheet

Work Sheet

NO.	ACCOUNT TITLES	ADJUSTED TRIAL BALANCE		AMOUNTS FOR CLOSING ENTRIES		POST-CLOSING TRIAL BALANCE	
		DR	CR	DR	CR	DR	CR

GENERAL JOURNAL

Date	Account Titles and Explanation	P. R.	Debit	Credit

Financial Statement Changes:

_____
_____
_____
_____
_____
_____
_____
_____
_____
_____

Problem 4-4A or 4-4B
Part 1

_____
_____

Income Statement

_____
_____
_____
_____
_____
_____
_____
_____
_____
_____
_____
_____
_____
_____
_____
_____
_____
_____
_____
_____
_____

Statement of Owner's Equity

Balance Sheet

GENERAL JOURNAL

Date	Account Titles and Explanation	P. R.	Debit	Credit

(a) _____

_____

_____

(b) _____

_____

_____

(c) _____

_____

_____

(d) _____

_____

_____

_____

Name _____

Work Sheet

NO.	Account Title	Unadjusted Trial Balance		Adjustments		Adjusted Trial Balance		Income Statement		Balance Sheet and Statement of Owner's Equity	
		Dr.	Cr.	Dr.	Cr.	Dr.	Cr.	Dr.	Cr.	Dr.	Cr.

GENERAL JOURNAL

Date	Account Titles and Explanation	P. R.	Debit	Credit

Chapter 4   Problem 4-5A or 4-5B   Name _____
Part 2   (Continued)
Closing Entries

GENERAL JOURNAL

Date	Account Titles and Explanation	P. R.	Debit	Credit

Income Statement

Statement of Owner's Equity

Balance Sheet

(a)

_____
_____
_____
_____
_____
_____
_____
_____
_____
_____
_____
_____
_____
_____

(b)

_____
_____
_____
_____
_____
_____
_____
_____
_____

Part 1

Partial Work Sheet

Account Title	Unadjusted Trial Balance		Amounts for Adjustments		Adjusted Trial Balance	
	Dr.	Cr.	Dr.	Cr.	Dr.	Cr.

GENERAL JOURNAL

Date	Account Titles and Explanation	P. R.	Debit	Credit

GENERAL JOURNAL

Date	Account Titles and Explanation	P. R.	Debit	Credit

Part 4

GENERAL JOURNAL

Date	Account Titles and Explanation	P. R.	Debit	Credit

Name _____

GENERAL JOURNAL

Date	Account Titles and Explanation	P. R.	Debit	Credit

Name _____

GENERAL LEDGER

Cash   ACCOUNT NO. 101

Date	Explanation	P.R.	DEBIT	CREDIT	BALANCE
2004, Dec. 31	Balance				58,160

Accounts Receivable   ACCOUNT NO. 106

Date	Explanation	P.R.	DEBIT	CREDIT	BALANCE
2004, Dec. 31	Balance				5,668

Computer Supplies   ACCOUNT NO. 126

Date	Explanation	P.R.	DEBIT	CREDIT	BALANCE
2004, Dec. 31	Balance				580

Prepaid Insurance   ACCOUNT NO. 128

Date	Explanation	P.R.	DEBIT	CREDIT	BALANCE
2004, Dec. 31	Balance				1,665

Prepaid Rent   ACCOUNT NO. 131

Date	Explanation	P.R.	DEBIT	CREDIT	BALANCE
2004, Dec. 31	Balance				825

Name _____

Office Equipment — ACCOUNT NO. 163

Date	Explanation	P.R.	DEBIT	CREDIT	BALANCE
2004, Dec. 31	Balance				8,000

Accumulated Depreciation - Office Equipment — ACCOUNT NO. 164

Date	Explanation	P.R.	DEBIT	CREDIT	BALANCE
2004, Dec. 31	Balance				400

Computer Equipment — ACCOUNT NO. 167

Date	Explanation	P.R.	DEBIT	CREDIT	BALANCE
2004, Dec. 31	Balance				20,000

Accumulated Depreciation-Computer Equipment — ACCOUNT NO. 168

Date	Explanation	P.R.	DEBIT	CREDIT	BALANCE
2004, Dec. 31	Balance				1,250

Accounts Payable — ACCOUNT NO. 201

Date	Explanation	P.R.	DEBIT	CREDIT	BALANCE
2004, Dec. 31	Balance				1,100

Wages Payable — ACCOUNT NO. 210

Date	Explanation	P.R.	DEBIT	CREDIT	BALANCE
2004, Dec. 31	Balance				500

Name _____

Unearned Computer Services Revenue — ACCOUNT NO. 236

Date	Explanation	P.R.	DEBIT	CREDIT	BALANCE
2004, Dec. 31	Balance				1,500

K. Breeze, Capital — ACCOUNT NO. 301

Date	Explanation	P.R.	DEBIT	CREDIT	BALANCE
2004, Dec. 31	Balance				83,000

K. Breeze, Withdrawals — ACCOUNT NO. 302

Date	Explanation	P.R.	DEBIT	CREDIT	BALANCE
2004, Dec. 31	Balance				7,100

Computer Service Revenue — ACCOUNT NO. 403

Date	Explanation	P.R.	DEBIT	CREDIT	BALANCE
2004, Dec. 31	Balance				31,284

Depreciation Expense-Office Equipment — ACCOUNT NO. 612

Date	Explanation	P.R.	DEBIT	CREDIT	BALANCE
2004, Dec. 31	Balance				400

Depreciation Expense-Computer Equipment — ACCOUNT NO. 613

Date	Explanation	P.R.	DEBIT	CREDIT	BALANCE
2004, Dec. 31	Balance				1,250

Wages Expense — ACCOUNT NO. 623

Date	Explanation	P.R.	DEBIT	CREDIT	BALANCE
2004, Dec. 31	Balance				3,875

Insurance Expense — ACCOUNT NO. 637

Date	Explanation	P.R.	DEBIT	CREDIT	BALANCE
2004, Dec. 31	Balance				555

Rent Expense — ACCOUNT NO. 640

Date	Explanation	P.R.	DEBIT	CREDIT	BALANCE
2004, Dec. 31	Balance				2,475

Computer Supplies Expense — ACCOUNT NO. 652

Date	Explanation	P.R.	DEBIT	CREDIT	BALANCE
2004, Dec. 31	Balance				3,065

Advertising Expense — ACCOUNT NO. 655

Date	Explanation	P.R.	DEBIT	CREDIT	BALANCE
2004, Dec. 31	Balance				2,965

Mileage Expense — ACCOUNT NO. 676

Date	Explanation	P.R.	DEBIT	CREDIT	BALANCE
2004, Dec. 31	Balance				896

Miscellaneous Expense   ACCOUNT NO. 677

Date	Explanation	P.R.	DEBIT	CREDIT	BALANCE
2004, Dec. 31	Balance				250

Repairs Expense, Computer   ACCOUNT NO. 684

Date	Explanation	P.R.	DEBIT	CREDIT	BALANCE
2004, Dec. 31	Balance				1,305

Income Summary   ACCOUNT NO. 901

Date	Explanation	P.R.	DEBIT	CREDIT	BALANCE

Name _____

SUCCESS SYSTEMS
Post-Closing Trial Balance
December 31, 2004

(1) _____

_____

_____

_____

_____

(2) _____

_____

_____

_____

_____

_____

_____

_____

_____

_____

_____

(3) _____

_____

_____

_____

_____

(4) _____

_____

_____

(5) Roll On: _____

_____

_____

_____

_____

_____

_____

Name _____

(1) _____

_____

_____

_____

_____

_____

_____

_____

(2) _____

_____

_____

_____

_____

(3) _____

_____

_____

_____

_____

(4) _____

_____

_____

_____

(1) _____
_____
_____
_____
_____
_____
_____
_____
_____
_____
_____
_____
_____
_____

(2) _____
_____
_____
_____
_____
_____
_____
_____
_____
_____
_____
_____
_____

MEMORANDUM

TO:
FROM:
SUBJECT:
DATE:

_____

(1) _____
_____
_____
_____
_____
_____
_____

(2) _____
_____
_____
_____
_____
_____

(3) _____
_____
_____
_____
_____
_____

1.

Account Title	Trial Balance		Adjustments		Balance Sheet	
	Debit	Credit	Debit	Credit	Debit	Credit

2.

Account Title	Trial Balance		Adjustments		Balance Sheet	
	Debit	Credit	Debit	Credit	Debit	Credit

GENERAL JOURNAL

Date	Account Titles and Explanation	P. R.	Debit	Credit

3.

Account Title	Trial Balance		Adjustments		Income Statement	
	Debit	Credit	Debit	Credit	Debit	Credit

GENERAL JOURNAL

Date	Account Titles and Explanation	P.R.	Debit	Credit

4.

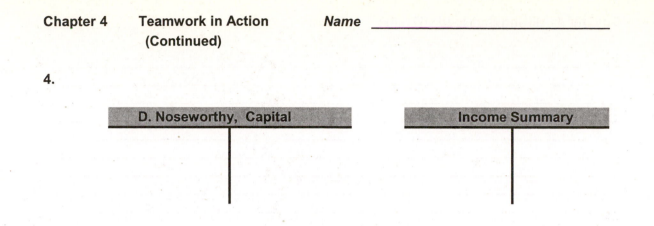

| D. Noseworthy, Capital | Income Summary |

GENERAL JOURNAL

Date	Account Titles and Explanation	P. R.	Debit	Credit

5. *Proving the Accounting Equation*

1. _____
_____
_____

2. _____
_____
_____

3. _____
_____
_____

4. _____
_____
_____

5. _____
_____
_____

Business Week Activity --BTN 4-8

(1) _____
_____
_____
_____

(2) _____
_____
_____
_____

(3) _____
_____
_____
_____

(4) _____
_____
_____
_____

(1) _____

_____

_____

_____

_____

_____

(2) _____

_____

_____

_____

_____

_____

(3) _____

_____

_____

_____

(4) _____

_____

_____

_____

_____

_____

Global Decision--BTN 4-10

1. _____

_____

_____

_____

2. _____

_____

_____

_____

Name _____

GENERAL JOURNAL

Date	Account Titles and Explanation	P. R.	Debit	Credit

GENERAL JOURNAL

Date	Account Titles and Explanation	P. R.	Debit	Credit

Case (a) _____

_____

_____

_____

_____

_____

Case (b) _____

_____

_____

_____

_____

Case (c) _____

_____

_____

_____

_____

_____

Case (d) _____

_____

_____

_____

_____

_____

Interpretation of (a) _____

_____

_____

_____

Quick Study 5-4

GENERAL JOURNAL

Date	Account Titles and Explanation	P. R.	Debit	Credit

GENERAL JOURNAL

Date	Account Titles and Explanation	P. R.	Debit	Credit

Quick Study 5-6:

Acid-Test Ratio: _____

_____

_____

_____

Interpretation: _____

_____

_____

_____

_____
_____
_____
_____
_____
_____
_____
_____
_____
_____
_____

Quick Study 5-8

(a) _____
(b) _____
(c) _____
(d) _____

GENERAL JOURNAL

Date		Account Titles and Explanation	P. R.	Debit	Credit

Quick Study 5-10

GENERAL JOURNAL

Date		Account Titles and Explanation	P. R.	Debit	Credit

Name _____

GENERAL JOURNAL

Date	Account Titles and Explanation	P. R.	Debit	Credit

(1) BUYER

GENERAL JOURNAL

Date	Account Titles and Explanation	P. R.	Debit	Credit

(2) SELLER

GENERAL JOURNAL

Date	Account Titles and Explanation	P. R.	Debit	Credit

(3)

_____
_____
_____
_____
_____
_____
_____
_____
_____
_____
_____
_____
_____
_____

Exercise 5-3

(1) _____	(6) _____
(2) _____	(7) _____
(3) _____	(8) _____
(4) _____	(9) _____
(5) _____	(10) _____

GENERAL JOURNAL

Date	Account Titles and Explanation	P. R.	Debit	Credit
Entries for Sale of Merchandise:				
Entries for (a):				
Entries for (b):				
Entries for (c):				

GENERAL JOURNAL

Date	Account Titles and Explanation	P. R.	Debit	Credit
Entries for Purchase of Merchandise:				
Entries for (a):				
Entries for (b):				
Entries for (c):				

(1) BUYER

GENERAL JOURNAL

Date		Account Titles and Explanation	P. R.	Debit	Credit

(1) SELLER

GENERAL JOURNAL

Date	Account Titles and Explanation	P. R.	Debit	Credit

Merchandise Inventory

Cost of Goods Sold

	(a)	(b)	(c)	(d)	(e)
Sales	$ 60,000	$ 42,500	$ 36,000		$ 23,600
Cost of goods sold					
Merchandise inventory (beg.)	6,000	17,050	7,500	7,000	2,560
Total cost of merch. purchases	36,000			32,000	5,600
Merchandise inventory (ending)		(2,700)	(9,000)	(6,600)	
Cost of goods sold	34,050	15,900			5,600
Gross profit			3,750	45,600	
Expenses	9,000	10,650	12,150	2,600	6,000
Net income (loss)		$ 15,950	$ (8,400)	$ 43,000	

Work space:

Exercise 5-10

Adjusting Entries:

GENERAL JOURNAL

Date	Account Titles and Explanation	P. R.	Debit	Credit

Closing Entries:

GENERAL JOURNAL

Date	Account Titles and Explanation	P. R.	Debit	Credit

Name _____

	Case X	Case Y	Case Z

Current Ratio

Acid-Test Ratio

Interpretation

Name _____

GENERAL JOURNAL

Date	Account Titles and Explanation	P. R.	Debit	Credit

(a) PERPETUAL

GENERAL JOURNAL

Date	Account Titles and Explanation	P. R.	Debit	Credit

Name _____

GENERAL JOURNAL

Date	Account Titles and Explanation	P. R.	Debit	Credit

(1) BUYER

GENERAL JOURNAL

Date	Account Titles and Explanation	P. R.	Debit	Credit

(2) SELLER

GENERAL JOURNAL

Date	Account Titles and Explanation	P. R.	Debit	Credit

Name _____

(1) BUYER

GENERAL JOURNAL

Date	Account Titles and Explanation	P. R.	Debit	Credit

(2) SELLER

GENERAL JOURNAL

Date	Account Titles and Explanation	P. R.	Debit	Credit

GENERAL JOURNAL

Date	Account Titles and Explanation	P. R.	Debit	Credit

GENERAL JOURNAL

Date	Account Titles and Explanation	P. R.	Debit	Credit

GENERAL JOURNAL

Date	Account Titles and Explanation	P. R.	Debit	Credit

GENERAL JOURNAL

Date	Account Titles and Explanation	P. R.	Debit	Credit

GENERAL JOURNAL

Date		Account Titles and Explanation	P. R.	Debit	Credit

Part 2

Income Statement

Income Statement

Part 4

_____
_____
_____
_____
_____
_____
_____
_____
_____
_____

Part 2

_____
_____
_____
_____
_____
_____
_____
_____
_____
_____

Income Statement

Part 4

Income Statement

GENERAL JOURNAL

Date		Account Titles and Explanation	P. R.	Debit	Credit

_____
_____
_____
_____

_____
_____
_____
_____

_____
_____
_____
_____

_____
_____
_____
_____

_____
_____
_____

Part 3

_____
_____
_____
_____

_____
_____
_____
_____

_____
_____
_____
_____

_____
_____

Chapter 5   Problem 5-6A or 5-6B

Name _____

_____, Company

Work Sheet

For Year Ended _____

Account Title	Unadjusted Trial Balance		Adjustments		Adjusted Trial Balance		Income Statement		Balance Sheet & Statement of Owner's Equity	
	Dr.	Cr.	Dr.	Cr.	Dr.	Cr.	Dr.	Cr.	Dr.	Cr.

Chapter 5   **Serial Problem**

Part 1   **Success Systems**

Journal Entries

Name _____

GENERAL JOURNAL

Date	Account Titles and Explanation	P. R.	Debit	Credit

Date	Account Titles and Explanation	P. R.	Debit	Credit

Date	Account Titles and Explanation	P. R.	Debit	Credit

Chapter 5   Serial Problem   Name _____
Part 1   Success Systems
Journal Entries   (Continued)

Date	Account Titles and Explanation	P. R.	Debit	Credit

Chapter 5   **Serial Problem**
Part 2   **Success Systems**
               (Continued)

Name _____

GENERAL LEDGER

Cash   **ACCOUNT NO. 101**

Date	Explanation	P.R.	DEBIT	CREDIT	BALANCE
2004 Dec. 31	Balance				58,160

Accounts Receivable - Alex's Engineering Co.   ACCOUNT NO. 106.1

Date	Explanation	P.R.	DEBIT	CREDIT	BALANCE
2004 Dec. 31	Balance				0

Accounts Receivable - Wildcat Services   ACCOUNT NO. 106.2

Date	Explanation	P.R.	DEBIT	CREDIT	BALANCE
2004 Dec. 31	Balance				0

Accounts Receivable - Easy Leasing   ACCOUNT NO. 106.3

Date	Explanation	P.R.	DEBIT	CREDIT	BALANCE
2004 Dec. 31	Balance				0

Accounts Receivable - Clark Co.   ACCOUNT NO. 106.4

Date	Explanation	P.R.	DEBIT	CREDIT	BALANCE
2004 Dec. 31	Balance				3,000

Chapter 5   **Serial Problem**
Part 2   **Success Systems**
          (Continued)

Name _____

Accounts Receivable - Chang Corporation   ACCOUNT NO. 106.5

Date	Explanation	P.R.	DEBIT	CREDIT	BALANCE
2004 Dec. 31	Balance				0

Accounts Receivable - Gomez Co.   ACCOUNT NO. 106.6

Date	Explanation	P.R.	DEBIT	CREDIT	BALANCE
2004 Dec. 31	Balance				2,668

Accounts Receivable - Delta Co.   ACCOUNT NO. 106.7

Date	Explanation	P.R.	DEBIT	CREDIT	BALANCE
2004 Dec. 31	Balance				0

Accounts Receivable - KC, Inc.   ACCOUNT NO. 106.8

Date	Explanation	P.R.	DEBIT	CREDIT	BALANCE
2004 Dec. 31	Balance				0

Accounts Receivable - Dream, Inc.   ACCOUNT NO. 106.9

Date	Explanation	P.R.	DEBIT	CREDIT	BALANCE
2004 Dec. 31	Balance				0

Name _____

	Merchandise Inventory				ACCOUNT NO. 119
Date	Explanation	P.R.	DEBIT	CREDIT	BALANCE
2004 Dec. 31	Balance				0

	Computer Supplies				ACCOUNT NO. 126
Date	Explanation	P.R.	DEBIT	CREDIT	BALANCE
2004 Dec. 31	Balance				580

	Prepaid Insurance				ACCOUNT NO. 128
Date	Explanation	P.R.	DEBIT	CREDIT	BALANCE
2004 Dec. 31	Balance				1,665

Name _____

Prepaid Rent   ACCOUNT NO. 131

Date	Explanation	P.R.	DEBIT	CREDIT	BALANCE
2004 Dec. 31	Balance				825

Office Equipment   ACCOUNT NO. 163

Date	Explanation	P.R.	DEBIT	CREDIT	BALANCE
2004 Dec. 31	Balance				8,000

Accumulated Depreciation - Office Equipment   ACCOUNT NO. 164

Date	Explanation	P.R.	DEBIT	CREDIT	BALANCE
2004 Dec. 31	Balance				400

Computer Equipment   ACCOUNT NO. 167

Date	Explanation	P.R.	DEBIT	CREDIT	BALANCE
2004 Dec. 31	Balance				20,000

Accumulated Depreciation - Computer Equipment   ACCOUNT NO. 168

Date	Explanation	P.R.	DEBIT	CREDIT	BALANCE
2004 Dec. 31	Balance				1,250

Name _____

Accounts Payable — ACCOUNT NO. 201

Date	Explanation	P.R.	DEBIT	CREDIT	BALANCE
2004 Dec. 31	Balance				1,100

Wages Payable — ACCOUNT NO. 210

Date	Explanation	P.R.	DEBIT	CREDIT	BALANCE
2004 Dec. 31	Balance				500

Unearned Computer Services Revenue — ACCOUNT NO. 236

Date	Explanation	P.R.	DEBIT	CREDIT	BALANCE
2004 Dec. 31	Balance				1,500

K. Breeze, Capital — ACCOUNT NO. 301

Date	Explanation	P.R.	DEBIT	CREDIT	BALANCE
2004 Dec. 31	Balance				90,148

K. Breeze, Withdrawals   ACCOUNT NO. 302

Date	Explanation	P.R.	DEBIT	CREDIT	BALANCE

Computer Services Revenue   ACCOUNT NO. 403

Date	Explanation	P.R.	DEBIT	CREDIT	BALANCE

Sales   ACCOUNT NO. 413

Date	Explanation	P.R.	DEBIT	CREDIT	BALANCE

Sales Returns and Allowances   ACCOUNT NO. 414

Date	Explanation	P.R.	DEBIT	CREDIT	BALANCE

Name _____

Sales Discounts   ACCOUNT NO. 415

Date	Explanation	P.R.	DEBIT	CREDIT	BALANCE

Cost of Goods Sold   ACCOUNT NO. 502

Date	Explanation	P.R.	DEBIT	CREDIT	BALANCE

Depreciation Expense-Office Equipment   ACCOUNT NO. 612

Date	Explanation	P.R.	DEBIT	CREDIT	BALANCE

Depreciation Expense-Computer Equipment   ACCOUNT NO. 613

Date	Explanation	P.R.	DEBIT	CREDIT	BALANCE

Wages Expense   ACCOUNT NO. 623

Date	Explanation	P.R.	DEBIT	CREDIT	BALANCE

Chapter 5   **Serial Problem**   *Name* _____
Part 2   **Success Systems**
                (Continued)

Insurance Expense   ACCOUNT NO. 637

Date	Explanation	P.R.	DEBIT	CREDIT	BALANCE

Rent Expense   ACCOUNT NO. 640

Date	Explanation	P.R.	DEBIT	CREDIT	BALANCE

Computer Supplies Expense   ACCOUNT NO. 652

Date	Explanation	P.R.	DEBIT	CREDIT	BALANCE

Advertising Expense   ACCOUNT NO. 655

Date	Explanation	P.R.	DEBIT	CREDIT	BALANCE

Mileage Expense   ACCOUNT NO. 676

Date	Explanation	P.R.	DEBIT	CREDIT	BALANCE

Miscellaneous Expense   ACCOUNT NO. 677

Date	Explanation	P.R.	DEBIT	CREDIT	BALANCE

Repairs Expense, Computer   ACCOUNT NO. 684

Date	Explanation	P.R.	DEBIT	CREDIT	BALANCE

SUCCESS SYSTEMS
Partial Work Sheet
March 31, 2005

Acct. No.	ACCOUNT TITLES	UNADJUSTED TRIAL BALANCE		ADJUSTMENTS		ADJUSTED TRIAL BALANCE	
		Dr.	Cr.	Dr.	Cr.	Dr.	Cr.

Chapter 5   **Serial Problem**
Part 4   **Success Systems**
             (Continued)

Name _____

SUCCESS SYSTEMS
Income Statement
For Three Months Ended March 31, 2005

Part 5

SUCCESS SYSTEMS
Statement of Owner's Equity
For Three Months Ended March 31, 2005

SUCCESS SYSTEMS
Balance Sheet
March 31, 2005

Part 1

_____
_____
_____
_____
_____
_____
_____
_____
_____

Part 2

_____
_____
_____
_____
_____
_____
_____
_____
_____
_____
_____
_____
_____
_____
_____

Part 3
Roll On: _____

_____
_____
_____
_____
_____
_____
_____
_____

Part 1

_____

_____

_____

_____

_____

_____

_____

_____

_____

_____

_____

_____

_____

_____

_____

_____

_____

_____

Part 2

_____

_____

_____

_____

_____

_____

Part 3

_____

_____

_____

_____

_____

_____

_____
_____
_____
_____
_____
_____
_____
_____
_____
_____
_____
_____
_____

Part 2

_____
_____
_____
_____
_____
_____
_____

MEMORANDUM

TO:

FROM:

SUBJECT:

DATE:

	2003	2002	2001	2000
Fiscal Year				
Revenues				
Cost of goods sold				
Gross margin				
Gross margin ratio				

Analysis: _____

(1a)

_____
_____
_____
_____
_____
_____
_____
_____
_____

(1b)

_____
_____
_____
_____
_____
_____
_____
_____
_____

(1c)

_____
_____
_____
_____
_____
_____
_____
_____
_____

(1d)

_____
_____
_____
_____
_____
_____
_____

_____

_____

_____

_____

_____

_____

_____

_____

(2)

Check: Net Income is _____ .

_____

(3)

_____

_____

_____

_____

_____

_____

_____

_____

(1) _____

_____

_____

_____

_____

(2) _____

_____

_____

_____

(3) _____

_____

_____

_____

(4) _____

_____

_____

_____

_____

(5) _____

_____

_____

_____

_____

_____

Damani Dada
Forecasted Income Statement
For Year Ended April 30, 2006

_____
_____
_____
_____
_____
_____
_____
_____

Part 2

_____
_____
_____
_____
_____
_____
_____
_____

Part 3

_____
_____
_____
_____
_____
_____
_____
_____
_____
_____
_____

_____

_____

_____

_____

_____

_____

_____

_____

_____

_____

_____

_____

_____

_____

_____

_____

_____

_____

_____

_____

_____

_____

_____

_____

(1) _____
_____
_____
_____
_____
_____
_____

(2) _____
_____
_____
_____
_____
_____

(3) _____
_____
_____
_____
_____
_____

a) FIFO

Date	Purchases	Cost of Goods Sold	Inventory Balance

b) LIFO

Date	Purchases	Cost of Goods Sold	Inventory Balance

c) Weighted Average

Date	Purchases	Cost of Goods Sold	Inventory Balance

d) Specific Identification

_____
_____
_____
_____
_____
_____
_____
_____
_____

Quick Study 6-3

b) FIFO

Date	Purchases	Cost of Goods Sold	Inventory Balance

c) LIFO

Date	Purchases	Cost of Goods Sold	Inventory Balance

c) Weighted Average

Date	Purchases	Cost of Goods Sold	Inventory Balance

Quick Study 6-4

(1) _____

(2) _____

(3) _____

(4) _____

(5) _____

Quick Study 6-5

(1) _____

_____

_____

(2) _____

_____

_____

_____
_____
_____
_____
_____

Quick Study 6-7

_____
_____
_____
_____
_____

Quick Study 6-8

_____
_____
_____
_____
_____

Quick Study 6-9

Inventory Items	Units	Per Unit		Total Cost	Total Market	LCM applied to:	
		Cost	Market			Items	Whole

(a) _____

(b) _____

(c) _____

(d) _____

(e) _____

(f) _____

Quick Study 6-11

_____

_____

_____

_____

_____

_____

_____

Quick Study 6-12^A

(a) _____

_____

(b) _____

_____

(c) _____

_____

(d) _____

_____

Chapter 6 Quick Study 6-13^{A} *Name* _____

(a) _____
_____
_____

(b) _____
_____

(c) _____
_____
_____

Quick Study 6-14^{B}

_____
_____
_____
_____
_____
_____
_____

Exercise 6-1
(a) Specific Identification

_____
_____
_____
_____
_____
_____
_____
_____

(b) Weighted Average Perpetual

Date	Purchases	Cost of Goods Sold	Inventory Balance

Name _____

(c) FIFO Perpetual

Date	Purchases	Cost of Goods Sold	Inventory Balance

(d) LIFO Perpetual

Date	Purchases	Cost of Goods Sold	Inventory Balance

Name _____

	Specific Identification	Weighted Average	FIFO	LIFO

LAKIA CORPORATION
Income Statements
For Year Ended December 31, 2005

(1) _____

_____

(2) _____

_____

(3) _____

_____

(a) FIFO Perpetual

Date	Purchases	Cost of Goods Sold	Inventory Balance

FIFO Gross Margin:

(a) LIFO Perpetual

Date	Purchases	Cost of Goods Sold	Inventory Balance

LIFO Gross Margin:

Specific Identification Method

(a) Ending Inventory and Cost of Goods Sold: _____
_____
_____
_____
_____
_____
_____
_____
_____
_____
_____
_____
_____
_____
_____
_____

(b) Gross Margin: _____
_____
_____
_____
_____
_____
_____

Inventory Items	Units	Per Unit		Total Cost	Total Market	LCM applied to:	
		Cost	Market			Products	Whole

(a) LCM applied to whole: _____

(b) LCM applied to products: _____

Exercise 6-6

(1) Gross Profit

_____

_____

_____

(2)

	2004	2005	2006
Sales			
Cost of goods sold:			
Beginning inventory			
Cost of Purchases			
Ending Inventory			
Cost of goods sold			
Gross Profit			

Inventory Turnover (2004): _____

_____

_____

_____

Inventory Turnover (2005): _____

_____

_____

_____

Days' Sales in Inventory (2004): _____

_____

_____

_____

Days' Sales in Inventory (2005): _____

_____

_____

_____

Analysis Comments: _____

_____

_____

_____

_____

(1) (a) _____

_____

_____

_____

_____

_____

(b) _____

_____

_____

_____

_____

_____

(2) _____

_____

_____

_____

_____

_____

_____

Method and Computations	Ending Inventory	Cost of Goods Sold
(a) Specific Identification		
(b) Weighted Average Periodic		
(c) FIFO Periodic		
(d) LIFO Periodic		

	Ending Inventory	Cost of Goods Sold
Method and Computations		
(a) FIFO Periodic		
(b) LIFO Periodic		
(c) FIFO Gross Margin:		
LIFO Gross Margin		

	Ending Inventory	Cost of Goods Sold
Method and Computations		
(a) **Specific Identification**		
(b) **Weighted Average Periodic**		
(c) **FIFO Periodic**		
(d) **LIFO Periodic**		

Income Effect(s):

Name _____

Method and Computations	Ending Inventory	Cost of Goods Sold
(a) Specific Identification		

(b) Weighted Average Periodic

(c) FIFO Periodic

(d) LIFO Periodic

Income Effect(s):

	At Cost	At Retail

Exercise 6-14^B

(1) Cost of Goods Available for Sale and Units Available for Sale:

_____

_____

_____

_____

_____

_____

_____

_____

_____

_____

_____

(2) Ending Inventory (in Units):

_____

_____

_____

_____

(3a) FIFO Perpetual

Date	Purchases	Cost of Goods Sold	Inventory Balance

(3b) LIFO Perpetual

Date	Purchases	Cost of Goods Sold	Inventory Balance

(3c) Specific Identification

(3d) Weighted Average Perpetual

Date	Purchases	Cost of Goods Sold	Inventory Balance

(4) Gross Profit

	FIFO	LIFO	Specific Identification	Weighted Average
Sales				
Cost of goods sold				
Gross profit				

(5) _____
_____
_____
_____
_____

Part 1

(a) Cost of Goods Sold	2004	2005	2006
Reported...........................			
Adjustments: 12/31/2004 error			
Adjustments: 12/31/2005 error			
Corrected...........................			

(b) Net Income	2004	2005	2006
Reported...........................			
Adjustments: 12/31/2004 error			
Adjustments: 12/31/2005 error			
Corrected...........................			

(c) Total Current Assets	2004	2005	2006
Reported...........................			
Adjustments: 12/31/2004 error			
Adjustments: 12/31/2005 error			
Corrected...........................			

(d) Equity	2004	2005	2006
Reported...........................			
Adjustments: 12/31/2004 error			
Adjustments: 12/31/2005 error			
Corrected...........................			

Part 2

_____
_____
_____
_____
_____
_____

Part 3

_____
_____
_____
_____
_____
_____
_____
_____

Inventory Items	Units	Per Unit		Total Cost	Total Market	LCM applied to :		
		Cost	Market			Items	Categories	Whole

(a) _____

_____

(b) _____

_____

(c) _____

_____

Chapter 6 Problem 6-4A or 6-4B   *Name* _____

Part 1

Units Available for Sale and Cost of Units Available for Sale: _____

_____

_____

_____

_____

_____

_____

_____

_____

_____

Part 2

(a) FIFO Periodic _____

_____

_____

_____

_____

_____

_____

_____

(b) LIFO Periodic _____

_____

_____

_____

_____

_____

_____

_____

_____

(C) Weighted Average Periodic _____

_____

_____

_____

_____

_____

_____

_____

Comparative Income Statements

Income Statements Comparing FIFO, LIFO and Weighted Average
For Year Ended December 31, 2005

	FIFO	LIFO	Weighted Average

Supporting Calculations:

_____

_____

_____

_____

_____

_____

_____

Part 3

Advantages:

    LIFO _____

_____

_____

    FIFO _____

_____

_____

Disadvantages:

    LIFO _____

_____

    FIFO _____

_____

_____ **Company**
Estimated Inventory
December 31

	At Cost	At Retail

Part 2

_____ **Company**
Inventory Shortage
December 31

	At Cost	At Retail

_____ Company Estimated Inventory March 31	At Cost	At Retail

Part 1

Inventory Turnover: _____
_____
_____

Days' Sales in Inventory: _____
_____
_____

Part 2

Analysis: _____
_____
_____
_____
_____

Reporting in Action--BTN 6-1

(1) _____
_____

(2) 2003: _____
_____
_____

     2002: _____
_____
_____

(3) _____
_____
_____
_____

(4) _____
_____
_____
_____
_____

(5)
(a) **Inventory Turnover:** _____
_____
_____
_____

(b) **Days' Sales in Inventory:** _____
_____
_____
_____

(6) **Roll On:** _____
_____
_____
_____
_____
_____
_____
_____
_____
_____
_____
_____
_____
_____

(1)
Inventory Turnover--Krispy Kreme: _____

_____

_____

_____

_____

Inventory Turnover--Tastykake:

_____

_____

_____

_____

_____

(2)
Days' Sales in Inventory - Krispy Kreme:

_____

_____

_____

_____

_____

_____

Days' Sales in Inventory - Tastykake:

_____

_____

_____

_____

_____

_____

_____

_____

(3) Interpretation: _____

_____

_____

_____

_____

_____

_____

_____

(1) Profit Margin: _____

_____

_____

_____

_____

Current Ratio: _____

_____

_____

_____

_____

(2) _____

_____

_____

_____

_____

_____

_____

_____

_____

_____

_____

MEMORANDUM
TO:
FROM:
SUBJECT:
DATE:

_____

_____

_____

_____

_____

_____

_____

_____

_____

_____

_____

_____

_____

_____

_____

_____

_____

_____

_____

_____

_____

_____

_____

_____

_____

_____

_____

_____

(1) _____

_____

(2) _____

_____

(3) Gross Margin: _____

_____

_____

Gross Margin Ratio: _____

(4) _____

Inventory Turnover: _____

_____

_____

Days' Sales in Inventory _____

_____

_____

_____

Teamwork in Action--BTN 6-6

(a) and (b) Concept discussion: _____

_____

_____

_____

_____

_____

_____

_____

_____

_____

_____

(a) and (b) Procedures:

Date	Purchases	Cost of Goods Sold	Inventory Balance

(c) _____

(d) _____

(e) _____

(1) _____

(2) _____

(3) _____

_____

_____

_____

_____

_____

(4) _____

_____

_____

Entrepreneurial Decision--BTN 6-8

(1)(a) _____

_____

_____

_____

_____

_____

_____

(b) _____

_____

_____

_____

_____

_____

_____

(2) _____

_____

_____

_____

_____

_____

_____

_____

_____
_____
_____
_____
_____
_____
_____
_____
_____
_____
_____
_____
_____
_____
_____
_____

Global Decision--BTN 6-10

(1) Inventory Turnover--Grupo Bimbo: _____
_____
_____
_____
_____

Days' Sales in Inventory--Grupo Bimbo: _____
_____
_____
_____
_____

(2) Interpretation: _____
_____
_____
_____
_____
_____

(1) _____

(2) _____

(3) _____

(4) _____

(5) _____

Quick Study 7-2

(1) _____

(2) _____

(3) _____

(4) _____

Quick Study 7-3

(1) _____   (7) _____

(2) _____   (8) _____

(3) _____   (9) _____

(4) _____   (10) _____

(5) _____   (11) _____

(6) _____   (12) _____

Quick Study 7-4

(a) _____

(b) _____

(c) _____

(d) _____

(e) _____

(f) _____

(g) _____

(h) _____

GENERAL JOURNAL

Date	Account Titles and Explanation	P. R.	Debit	Credit

Quick Study 7-6
Information Reportable: _____
_____
_____
_____

Exercise 7-1

SALES JOURNAL

Date	Account Debited	Invoice Number	PR	Accts. Rec. Dr. Sales Cr.	Cost of Goods Sold Dr. Inventory Cr.

Exercise 7-2
March 2 _____
   5 _____
   7 _____
   8 _____
  12 _____
  16 _____
  19 _____
  25 _____

SALES JOURNAL				
Date	Account Debited	Invoice Number	PR	Accts. Rec. Dr. Sales Cr.

Exercise 7-4

CASH RECEIPTS JOURNAL								
Date	Account Credited	Explanation	PR	Cash Dr.	Sales Discount Dr.	Accts. Rec. Cr.	Sales Cr.	Other Accts. Cr.	Cost of Goods Sold Dr. Inv. Cr.

Exercise 7-5

November 3	
7	
9	
13	
18	
22	
27	
30	

Exercise 7-6

CASH RECEIPTS JOURNAL							
Date	Account Credited	Explanation	PR	Cash Dr.	Sales Discount Dr.	Accts. Rec. Cr.	Sales Cr.	Other Accts. Cr.

PURCHASES JOURNAL								
Date	Account	Date of Invoice	Terms	PR	Accts. Payable Cr.	Inventory Dr.	Office Supplies Dr.	Other Accts. Dr.

Exercise 7-8

June	1	_____
	8	_____
	14	_____
	17	_____
	24	_____
	28	_____
	29	_____

Exercise 7-9

PURCHASES JOURNAL								
Date	Account	Date of Invoice	Terms	PR	Accts. Payable Cr.	Purchases Dr.	Office Supplies Dr.	Other Accts. Dr.

Exercise 7-10

CASH DISBURSEMENTS JOURNAL								
Date	Ck. No.	Payee	Account Debited	PR	Cash Cr.	Inventory Cr.	Other Accts. Dr.	Accts. Payable Dr.

April	3	_____
	9	_____
	12	_____
	17	_____
	20	_____
	29	_____
	30	_____
	31	_____

Exercise 7-12

			CASH DISBURSEMENTS JOURNAL					
Date	Ck. No.	Payee	Account Debited	PR	Cash Cr.	Purchases Discounts Cr.	Other Accts. Dr.	Accts. Payable Dr.

Exercise 7-13

(a) _____

_____

_____

(b) _____

_____

_____

Name _____

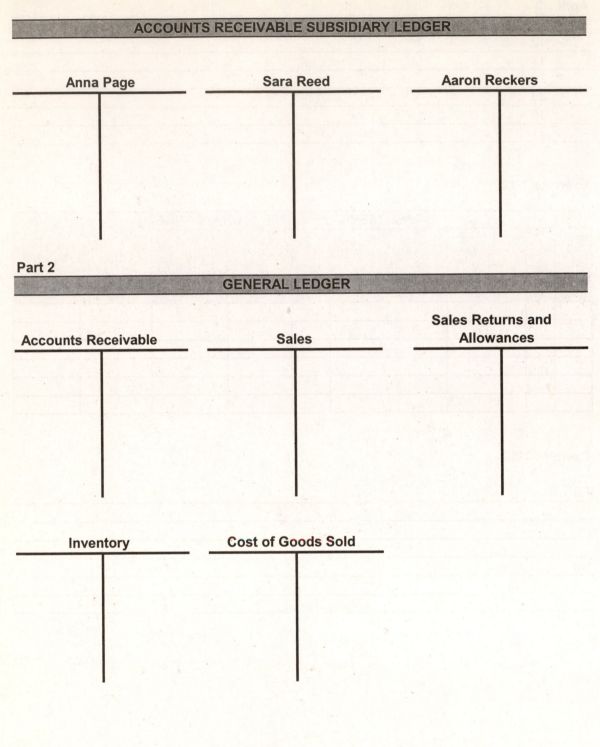

ACCOUNTS RECEIVABLE SUBSIDIARY LEDGER

Anna Page

Sara Reed

Aaron Reckers

Part 2

GENERAL LEDGER

Accounts Receivable

Sales

Sales Returns and Allowances

Inventory

Cost of Goods Sold

Schedule of Accounts Receivable

Accounts Receivable Controlling Account

ACCOUNTS RECEIVABLE LEDGER

Eric Horner

Hong Jiang

Joe Mack

Tess Cox

Part 2

GENERAL LEDGER

Accounts Receivable

Sales

Part 3

Schedule of Accounts Receivable

(1) _____

(2) _____

(3) _____

(4) _____

(5) _____

Exercise 7-17

Segment	Segment Income (in $ mil.)		Segment Assets (in %)		Segment Return on Assets
	2004	2003	2004	2003	2004

Analysis and Interpretation:

Sales Journal					Page 3
Date	Account Debited	Invoice Number	PR	Accts. Receivable Dr. Sales Cr.	Cost of Goods Sold Dr. Inventory Cr.

Cash Receipts Journal									Page 3
Date	Account Credited	Explanation	PR	Cash Dr.	Sales Disc. Dr.	Accts. Rec. Cr.	Sales Cr.	Other Accts. Cr.	Cost of Goods Sold Dr. Inv. Cr.

GENERAL LEDGER

Cash   ACCOUNT NO. 101

Date	Explanation	P.R.	DEBIT	CREDIT	BALANCE

Accounts Receivable   ACCOUNT NO. 106

Date	Explanation	P.R.	DEBIT	CREDIT	BALANCE

Inventory   ACCOUNT NO. 119

Date	Explanation	P.R.	DEBIT	CREDIT	BALANCE

Long-Term Notes Payable   ACCOUNT NO. 251

Date	Explanation	P.R.	DEBIT	CREDIT	BALANCE

Sales   ACCOUNT NO. 413

Date	Explanation	P.R.	DEBIT	CREDIT	BALANCE

Sales Discounts   ACCOUNT NO. 415

Date	Explanation	P.R.	DEBIT	CREDIT	BALANCE

	Cost of Goods Sold				ACCOUNT NO. 502
Date	Explanation	P.R.	DEBIT	CREDIT	BALANCE

ACCOUNTS RECEIVABLE LEDGER

Date	Explanation	P.R.	DEBIT	CREDIT	BALANCE

Date	Explanation	P.R.	DEBIT	CREDIT	BALANCE

Date	Explanation	P.R.	DEBIT	CREDIT	BALANCE

Trial Balance

Schedule of Accounts Receivable

Part 5

Analysis:

Sales Journal				Page 3
Date	Account Debited	Invoice Number	PR	Accts Receivable Dr. Sales Cr.

Cash Receipts Journal								Page 3
Date	Account Credited	Explanation	PR	Cash Dr.	Sales Discount Dr.	Accts. Rec. Cr.	Sales Cr.	Other Accts. Cr.

GENERAL LEDGER

Cash   ACCOUNT NO. 101

Date	Explanation	P.R.	DEBIT	CREDIT	BALANCE

Accounts Receivable   ACCOUNT NO. 106

Date	Explanation	P.R.	DEBIT	CREDIT	BALANCE

Inventory   ACCOUNT NO. 119

Date	Explanation	P.R.	DEBIT	CREDIT	BALANCE

Long-Term Notes Payable   ACCOUNT NO. 251

Date	Explanation	P.R.	DEBIT	CREDIT	BALANCE

Sales   ACCOUNT NO. 413

Date	Explanation	P.R.	DEBIT	CREDIT	BALANCE

Sales Discounts   ACCOUNT NO. 415

Date	Explanation	P.R.	DEBIT	CREDIT	BALANCE

ACCOUNTS RECEIVABLE LEDGER

Date	Explanation	P.R.	DEBIT	CREDIT	BALANCE

Date	Explanation	P.R.	DEBIT	CREDIT	BALANCE

Date	Explanation	P.R.	DEBIT	CREDIT	BALANCE

Trial Balance

Schedule of Accounts Receivable

Part 5

Analysis Component:

Name _____

Purchases Journal   Page 3

Date	Account	Date of Invoice	Terms	PR	Accts. Payable Cr.	Inventory Dr.	Office Supplies Dr.	Other Accts. Dr.

Cash Disbursements Journal   Page 3

Date	Ck. No.	Payee	Account Debited	PR	Cash Cr.	Inventory Cr.	Other Accts. Dr.	Accts. Payable Dr.

GENERAL JOURNAL   Page 3

Date		Account Titles and Explanation	P. R.	Debit	Credit

GENERAL LEDGER

Cash   ACCOUNT NO. 101

Date	Explanation	P.R.	DEBIT	CREDIT	BALANCE

Inventory   ACCOUNT NO. 119

Date	Explanation	P.R.	DEBIT	CREDIT	BALANCE

Office Supplies   ACCOUNT NO. 124

Date	Explanation	P.R.	DEBIT	CREDIT	BALANCE

Store Supplies   ACCOUNT NO. 125

Date	Explanation	P.R.	DEBIT	CREDIT	BALANCE

Store Equipment   ACCOUNT NO. 165

Date	Explanation	P.R.	DEBIT	CREDIT	BALANCE

Accounts Payable   ACCOUNT NO. 201

Date	Explanation	P.R.	DEBIT	CREDIT	BALANCE

Long-Term Notes Payable   ACCOUNT NO. 251

Date	Explanation	P.R.	DEBIT	CREDIT	BALANCE

Sales Salaries Expense   ACCOUNT NO. 621

Date	Explanation	P.R.	DEBIT	CREDIT	BALANCE

Advertising Expense   ACCOUNT NO. 655

Date	Explanation	P.R.	DEBIT	CREDIT	BALANCE

ACCOUNTS PAYABLE LEDGER

_____

Date	Explanation	P.R.	DEBIT	CREDIT	BALANCE

_____

Date	Explanation	P.R.	DEBIT	CREDIT	BALANCE

_____

Date	Explanation	P.R.	DEBIT	CREDIT	BALANCE

ACCOUNTS PAYABLE LEDGER

Date	Explanation	P.R.	DEBIT	CREDIT	BALANCE

Part 4

Trial Balance

Schedule of Accounts Payable

Purchases Journal								Page 3
Date	Account	Date of Invoice	Terms	PR	Accts. Payable Cr.	Purchases Dr.	Office Supplies Dr.	Other Accts. Dr.

Cash Disbursements Journal								Page 3
Date	Ck. No.	Payee	Account Debited	PR	Cash Cr.	Purchases Discount Cr.	Other Accts. Dr.	Accts. Payable Dr.

GENERAL JOURNAL   Page 3

Date	Account Titles and Explanation	P. R.	Debit	Credit

GENERAL LEDGER

Cash   ACCOUNT NO. 101

Date	Explanation	P.R.	DEBIT	CREDIT	BALANCE

Inventory   ACCOUNT NO. 119

Date	Explanation	P.R.	DEBIT	CREDIT	BALANCE

Office Supplies   ACCOUNT NO. 124

Date	Explanation	P.R.	DEBIT	CREDIT	BALANCE

Store Supplies   ACCOUNT NO. 125

Date	Explanation	P.R.	DEBIT	CREDIT	BALANCE

Store Equipment   ACCOUNT NO. 165

Date	Explanation	P.R.	DEBIT	CREDIT	BALANCE

Accounts Payable   ACCOUNT NO. 201

Date	Explanation	P.R.	DEBIT	CREDIT	BALANCE

Long-Term Notes Payable   ACCOUNT NO. 251

Date	Explanation	P.R.	DEBIT	CREDIT	BALANCE

Purchases   ACCOUNT NO. 505

Date	Explanation	P.R.	DEBIT	CREDIT	BALANCE

Purchase Returns and Allowances   ACCOUNT NO. 506

Date	Explanation	P.R.	DEBIT	CREDIT	BALANCE

Purchase Discounts   ACCOUNT NO. 507

Date	Explanation	P.R.	DEBIT	CREDIT	BALANCE

Sales Salaries Expense   ACCOUNT NO. 621

Date	Explanation	P.R.	DEBIT	CREDIT	BALANCE

Advertising Expense   ACCOUNT NO. 655

Date	Explanation	P.R.	DEBIT	CREDIT	BALANCE

ACCOUNTS PAYABLE LEDGER

Date	Explanation	P.R.	DEBIT	CREDIT	BALANCE

Date	Explanation	P.R.	DEBIT	CREDIT	BALANCE

Date	Explanation	P.R.	DEBIT	CREDIT	BALANCE

Date	Explanation	P.R.	DEBIT	CREDIT	BALANCE

Trial Balance

Schedule of Accounts Payable

Name _____

				Sales Journal		Page 3
Date	Account Debited	Invoice Number	PR	Accts Rec. Dr. Sales Cr.	Cost of Goods Sold Dr. Inventory Cr.	
Dec. 6	Marge Craig	913	√	3,300	1,500	
12	Hanna Seppa	914	√	3,650	2,850	
15	Bo Brown	915	√	3,100	1,800	

					Purchases Journal			Page 3
Date	Account	Date of Inv.	Terms	PR	Accts. Pay. Cr.	Inventory Dr.	Office Supplies Dr.	Other Accts. Dr.
Dec. 2	Funk Co.	12/2	2/10, n/30	√	3,200	3,200		
5	KK's Supply Co.	12/3	n/10, EOM	√	1,300	1,300		
15	Funk Co.	12/15	2/10, n/60	√	3,990	3,990		
15	Crossland Co.	12/15	2/10, n/60	√	2,650	2,650		

				Cash Receipts Journal					Page 3
Date	Account Credited	Explanation	PR	Cash Dr.	Sales Disc Dr.	Accts. Rec. Cr.	Sales Cr.	Other Accts. Cr.	Cost of Goods Sold Dr. Inv. Cr.
Dec.2	Shilo Jones	Inv. 11/23	√	4,116	84	4,200			
15	Sales	Cash sales	√	38,830			38,830		19,800
15	Marge Craig	Inv. 12/6	√	2,401	49	2,450			

			Cash Disbursements Jounral					Page 4
Date	Ck. No.	Payee	Account Debited	PR	Cash Cr.	Inv. Cr.	Other Accts. Dr.	Accts. Payable Dr.
Dec. 2	619	Omni Realty Co.	Rent Exp.	640	2,250		2,250	
6	620	Fireside Co.	Fireside Co.	√	3,724	76		3,800
12	621	Funk Co.	Funk Co.	√	3,136	64		3,200
15	622	Jamie Inman	Sales Salaries Exp.	621	2,020		2,020	

GENERAL JOURNAL   Page 2

Date		Account Titles and Explanation	P. R.	Debit	Credit
Dec.	4	Accounts Payable --Fireside Co.	201/√	460	
		Inventory	119		460
		Received a credit memo for returns.			
Dec.	9	Sales Returns and Allowances	414	850	
		Accounts Receivable--M.Craig	106/√		850
		Issued a credit memorandum			

GENERAL LEDGER

Cash   ACCOUNT NO. 101

Date	Explanation	P.R.	DEBIT	CREDIT	BALANCE
Nov. 30	Balance				5,361

Accounts Receivable   ACCOUNT NO. 106

Date	Explanation	P.R.	DEBIT	CREDIT	BALANCE
Nov. 30	Balance				4,200
Dec. 9		G2		850	3,350

Merchandise Inventory   ACCOUNT NO. 119

Date	Explanation	P.R.	DEBIT	CREDIT	BALANCE
Nov. 30	Balance				66,970
Dec. 4		G2		460	66,510

Office Supplies   ACCOUNT NO. 124

Date	Explanation	P.R.	DEBIT	CREDIT	BALANCE
Nov. 30	Balance				607

Store Supplies   ACCOUNT NO. 125

Date	Explanation	P.R.	DEBIT	CREDIT	BALANCE
Nov. 30	Balance				346

Store Equipment   ACCOUNT NO. 165

Date	Explanation	P.R.	DEBIT	CREDIT	BALANCE
Nov. 30	Balance				42,129

Accumulated Depreciation-Store Equipment   ACCOUNT NO. 166

Date	Explanation	P.R.	DEBIT	CREDIT	BALANCE
Nov. 30	Balance				9,153

Accounts Payable   ACCOUNT NO. 201

Date	Explanation	P.R.	DEBIT	CREDIT	BALANCE
Nov. 30	Balance				4,260
Dec. 4		G2	460		3,800

Ken Choi, Capital   ACCOUNT NO. 308

Date	Explanation	P.R.	DEBIT	CREDIT	BALANCE
Nov. 30	Balance				106,200

Ken Choi, Withdrawals   ACCOUNT NO. 318

Date	Explanation	P.R.	DEBIT	CREDIT	BALANCE

Sales   ACCOUNT NO. 413

Date	Explanation	P.R.	DEBIT	CREDIT	BALANCE

Sales Returns and Allowances   ACCOUNT NO. 414

Date	Explanation	P.R.	DEBIT	CREDIT	BALANCE
Dec. 9		G2	850		850

Sales Discounts   ACCOUNT NO. 415

Date	Explanation	P.R.	DEBIT	CREDIT	BALANCE

Cost of Goods Sold   ACCOUNT NO. 502

Date	Explanation	P.R.	DEBIT	CREDIT	BALANCE

Sales Salaries Expense   ACCOUNT NO. 621

Date	Explanation	P.R.	DEBIT	CREDIT	BALANCE
Dec.15		D4	2,020		2,020

Rent Expense   ACCOUNT NO. 640

Date	Explanation	P.R.	DEBIT	CREDIT	BALANCE
Dec. 2		D4	2,250		2,250

Utilities Expense					ACCOUNT NO. 690
Date	Explanation	P.R.	DEBIT	CREDIT	BALANCE

ACCOUNTS RECEIVABLE LEDGER

Marge Craig

Date	Explanation	P.R.	DEBIT	CREDIT	BALANCE
Dec. 6		S3	3,300		3,300
9		G2		850	2,450
15		R3		2,450	0

Hanna Seppa

Date	Explanation	P.R.	DEBIT	CREDIT	BALANCE
Dec. 12		S3	3,650		3,650

Shilo Jones

Date	Explanation	P.R.	DEBIT	CREDIT	BALANCE
Nov. 23		S3	4,200		4,200
Dec. 2		R3		4,200	0

Bo Brown

Date	Explanation	P.R.	DEBIT	CREDIT	BALANCE
Dec.15		S3	3,100		3,100

ACCOUNTS PAYABLE LEDGER

Fireside Company

Date	Explanation	P.R.	DEBIT	CREDIT	BALANCE
Nov. 28		P2		4,260	4,260
Dec. 4		G2	460		3,800
6		D4	3,800		0

KK's Supply Company

Date	Explanation	P.R.	DEBIT	CREDIT	BALANCE
Dec. 5		P2		1,300	1,300

Crossland Company

Date	Explanation	P.R.	DEBIT	CREDIT	BALANCE
Dec. 15		P2		2,650	2,650

Funk Company

Date	Explanation	P.R.	DEBIT	CREDIT	BALANCE
Dec. 2		P2		3,200	3,200
12		D4	3,200		0
15		P2		3,990	3,990

| CHOI ENTERPRISES |
| Trial Balance |
| December 31 |

| CHOI ENTERPRISES |
| Schedule of Accounts Receivable |
| December 31 |

CHOI ENTERPRISES
Schedule of Accounts Payable
December 31

_____
_____
_____
_____
_____
_____

Problem 7-5B
Parts 1 and 2

	SALES JOURNAL				Page 3
Date	Account Debited	Invoice Number	PR	Accts Rec. Dr. Sales Cr.	Cost of Goods Sold Dr. Inventory Cr.
Dec. 6	Marge Craig	913	√	3,300	1,780
12	Brad Sills	914	√	3,650	1,958
15	Leslie Wilson	915	√	3,100	1,845

Purchase Journal								Page 2
Date	Account	Date of Inv.	Terms	PR	Accts. Pay. Cr.	Inventory Dr.	Office Supplies Dr.	Other Accts. Dr.
Dec. 2	Chiefs Co.	12/2	2/10, n/60	√	3,200	3,200		
5	Black Supply Co.	12/3	n/10,EOM	√	1,300	1,300		
15	Chiefs Co.	12/15	2/10,n/60	√	3,990	3,990		
15	Blue Co.	12/15	2/10, n/60	√	2,650	2,650		

Cash Receipts Journal								Page 3
Date	Account Credited	Explanation	PR	Cash Dr.	Sales Disc. Dr.	Accts. Rec. Cr.	Sales Cr.	Other Accts. Cr.	Cost of Goods Sold Dr. Inv. Cr.
Dec. 2	Mo Carp	Inv. 11/23	√	4,116	84	4,200			
15	Sales	Cash sales	√	38,830			38,830		20,122
15	Marge Craig	Inv. 12/6	√	2,401	49	2,450			

Cash Disbursements Journal								PAGE 4
Date	Ck. No.	Payee	Account Debited	PR	Cash Cr.	Inventory Cr.	Other Accts. Dr.	Accts. Payable Dr.
Dec. 2	619	Omni Realty Co.	Rent Exp.	640	2,250		2,250	
6	620	Fireside Co.	Fireside Co.	√	3,724	76		3,800
12	621	Chiefs Co.	Chiefs Co.	√	3,136	64		3,200
15	622	Sue Hart	Sales Salaries Exp.	621	2,620		2,620	

GENERAL JOURNAL   Page 2

Date		Account Titles and Explanation	P. R.	Debit	Credit
Dec.	4	Accounts Payable - Fireside Co.	210/√	460	
		Inventory	119		460
		Received a credit memo for returns.			
	9	Sales Returns and Allowances	414	850	
		Accounts Receivable-M. Craig	106/√		850
		Issued a credit memorandum.			

GENERAL LEDGER

Cash   ACCOUNT NO. 101

Date	Explanation	P.R.	DEBIT	CREDIT	BALANCE
Nov. 30	Balance				5,361

Accounts Receivable   ACCOUNT NO. 106

Date	Explanation	P.R.	DEBIT	CREDIT	BALANCE
Nov. 30	Balance				4,200
Dec. 9		G2		850	3,350

Merchandise Inventory   ACCOUNT NO. 119

Date	Explanation	P.R.	DEBIT	CREDIT	BALANCE
Nov. 30	Balance				66,970
Dec. 4		G2		460	66,510

Office Supplies   ACCOUNT NO. 124

Date	Explanation	P.R.	DEBIT	CREDIT	BALANCE
Nov. 30	Balance				607

Store Supplies   ACCOUNT NO. 125

Date	Explanation	P.R.	DEBIT	CREDIT	BALANCE
Nov. 30	Balance				346

Store Equipment   ACCOUNT NO. 165

Date	Explanation	P.R.	DEBIT	CREDIT	BALANCE
Nov. 30	Balance				42,129

Accumulated Depreciation-Store Equipment   ACCOUNT NO. 166

Date	Explanation	P.R.	DEBIT	CREDIT	BALANCE
Nov. 30	Balance				9,153

Accounts Payable   ACCOUNT NO. 201

Date	Explanation	P.R.	DEBIT	CREDIT	BALANCE
Nov. 30	Balance				4,260
Dec. 4		G2	460		3,800

S. Morris , Capital   ACCOUNT NO. 308

Date	Explanation	P.R.	DEBIT	CREDIT	BALANCE
Nov. 30	Balance				106,200

S. Morris, Withdrawals   ACCOUNT NO. 318

Date	Explanation	P.R.	DEBIT	CREDIT	BALANCE

Name _____

Sales — ACCOUNT NO. 413

Date	Explanation	P.R.	DEBIT	CREDIT	BALANCE

Sales Returns and Allowances — ACCOUNT NO. 414

Date	Explanation	P.R.	DEBIT	CREDIT	BALANCE
Dec. 9		G2	850		850

Sales Discounts — ACCOUNT NO. 415

Date	Explanation	P.R.	DEBIT	CREDIT	BALANCE

Cost of Goods Sold — ACCOUNT NO. 502

Date	Explanation	P.R.	DEBIT	CREDIT	BALANCE

Sales Salaries Expense — ACCOUNT NO. 621

Date	Explanation	P.R.	DEBIT	CREDIT	BALANCE
Dec.15	Balance	D4	2620		2,620

Rent Expense — ACCOUNT NO. 640

Date	Explanation	P.R.	DEBIT	CREDIT	BALANCE
Dec. 2		D4			2,250

Utilities Expense					ACCOUNT NO. 690
Date	Explanation	P.R.	DEBIT	CREDIT	BALANCE

ACCOUNTS RECEIVABLE LEDGER

Marge Craig

Date	Explanation	P.R.	DEBIT	CREDIT	BALANCE
Dec. 6		S3	3,300		3,300
9		G2		850	2,450
15		R3		2,450	0

Brad Sills

Date	Explanation	P.R.	DEBIT	CREDIT	BALANCE
Dec.12		S3	3,650		3,650

Leslie Wilson

Date	Explanation	P.R.	DEBIT	CREDIT	BALANCE
Dec. 15		S3	3,100		3,100

Mo Carp

Date	Explanation	P.R.	DEBIT	CREDIT	BALANCE
Nov 23		S3	4,200		4,200
Dec. 2		R3		4,200	0

ACCOUNTS PAYABLE LEDGER

Fireside Company

Date	Explanation	P.R.	DEBIT	CREDIT	BALANCE
Nov. 28		P1		4,260	4,260
Dec. 4		G2	460		3,800
6		D4	3,800		0

Black Supply Company

Date	Explanation	P.R.	DEBIT	CREDIT	BALANCE
Dec. 5		P2		1,300	1,300

Blue Company

Date	Explanation	P.R.	DEBIT	CREDIT	BALANCE
Dec.15		P2		2,650	2,650

Chiefs Company

Date	Explanation	P.R.	DEBIT	CREDIT	BALANCE
Dec. 2		P2		3,200	3200
12		D4	3,200		0
15		P2		3,990	3990

Name ______________________

YES PRODUCTS
Trial Balance
December 31

YES PRODUCTS
Schedule of Accounts Receivable
December 31

YES PRODUCTS
Schedule of Accounts Payable
December 31

_____

_____

_____

_____

_____

_____

_____

Problem 7-6A or 7-6B
Parts 1 and 2

Sales Journal					Page 2
Date	Account Debited	Invoice Number	PR	Accts. Rec. Dr. Sales Cr.	Cost of Goods Sold Dr. Inventory Cr.

Cash Receipts Journal									Page 2
Date	Account Credited	Explanation	PR	Cash Dr.	Sales Disc. Dr.	Accts. Rec. Cr.	Sales Cr.	Other Accts. Cr.	Cost of Goods Sold Dr. Inv. Cr.

					Purchase Journal			Page 2
Date	Account	Date of Inv.	Terms	PR	Accts. Pay. Cr.	Inventory Dr.	Office Supplies Dr.	Other Accts. Dr.

				Cash Disbursements Journal				Page 2
Date	Ck. No.	Payee	Account Debited	PR	Cash Cr.	Inventory Cr.	Other Accts. Dr.	Accts. Payable Dr.

GENERAL JOURNAL   Page 2

Date	Account Titles and Explanation	P. R.	Debit	Credit

GENERAL LEDGER

Cash   ACCOUNT NO. 101

Date	Explanation	P.R.	DEBIT	CREDIT	BALANCE

Accounts Receivable   ACCOUNT NO. 106

Date	Explanation	P.R.	DEBIT	CREDIT	BALANCE

Inventory   ACCOUNT NO. 119

Date	Explanation	P.R.	DEBIT	CREDIT	BALANCE

Office Supplies   ACCOUNT NO. 124

Date	Explanation	P.R.	DEBIT	CREDIT	BALANCE

Store Supplies   ACCOUNT NO. 125

Date	Explanation	P.R.	DEBIT	CREDIT	BALANCE

Office Equipment   ACCOUNT NO. 163

Date	Explanation	P.R.	DEBIT	CREDIT	BALANCE

Accounts Payable   ACCOUNT NO. 201

Date	Explanation	P.R.	DEBIT	CREDIT	BALANCE

Long-Term Notes Payable   ACCOUNT NO. 251

Date	Explanation	P.R.	DEBIT	CREDIT	BALANCE

, Capital   ACCOUNT NO. 308

Date	Explanation	P.R.	DEBIT	CREDIT	BALANCE

Sales   ACCOUNT NO. 413

Date	Explanation	P.R.	DEBIT	CREDIT	BALANCE

Sales Discounts   ACCOUNT NO. 415

Date	Explanation	P.R.	DEBIT	CREDIT	BALANCE

Cost of Goods Sold   ACCOUNT NO. 502

Date	Explanation	P.R.	DEBIT	CREDIT	BALANCE

Sales Salaries Expense   **ACCOUNT NO. 621**

Date	Explanation	P.R.	DEBIT	CREDIT	BALANCE

ACCOUNTS RECEIVABLE LEDGER

Date	Explanation	P.R.	DEBIT	CREDIT	BALANCE

Date	Explanation	P.R.	DEBIT	CREDIT	BALANCE

Date	Explanation	P.R.	DEBIT	CREDIT	BALANCE

ACCOUNTS PAYABLE LEDGER

Date	Explanation	P.R.	DEBIT	CREDIT	BALANCE

Date	Explanation	P.R.	DEBIT	CREDIT	BALANCE

Date	Explanation	P.R.	DEBIT	CREDIT	BALANCE

Date	Explanation	P.R.	DEBIT	CREDIT	BALANCE

Trial Balance

Schedule of Accounts Receivable

Schedule of Accounts Payable

				Sales Journal		Page 2
Date	Account Debited		Invoice Number	PR	Accts. Receivable Dr. Sales Cr.	

				Cash Receipts Journal				Page 2
Date	Account Credited	Explanation	PR	Cash Dr.	Sales Disc. Dr.	Accts. Rec. Cr.	Sales Cr.	Other Accts. Cr.

								Purchases Journal							Page 2

Date	Account	Date of Inv.	Terms	PR	Accts. Payable Cr.	Purchases Dr.	Office Supplies Dr.	Other Accts. Dr.

				Cash Disbursements Journal					Page 2

Date	Ck. No.	Payee	Account Debited	PR	Cash Cr.	Purch. Disc. Cr.	Other Accts. Dr.	Accts. Payable Dr.

GENERAL JOURNAL   Page 2

Date	Account Titles and Explanation	P. R.	Debit	Credit

GENERAL LEDGER

Cash   ACCOUNT NO. 101

Date	Explanation	P.R.	DEBIT	CREDIT	BALANCE

Accounts Receivable   ACCOUNT NO. 106

Date	Explanation	P.R.	DEBIT	CREDIT	BALANCE

Inventory   ACCOUNT NO. 119

Date	Explanation	P.R.	DEBIT	CREDIT	BALANCE

Office Supplies   ACCOUNT NO. 124

Date	Explanation	P.R.	DEBIT	CREDIT	BALANCE

Store Supplies   ACCOUNT NO. 125

Date	Explanation	P.R.	DEBIT	CREDIT	BALANCE

Office Equipment   ACCOUNT NO. 163

Date	Explanation	P.R.	DEBIT	CREDIT	BALANCE

Accounts Payable   ACCOUNT NO. 201

Date	Explanation	P.R.	DEBIT	CREDIT	BALANCE

Long-Term Notes Payable   ACCOUNT NO. 251

Date	Explanation	P.R.	DEBIT	CREDIT	BALANCE

, Capital   ACCOUNT NO. 308

Date	Explanation	P.R.	DEBIT	CREDIT	BALANCE

Sales   ACCOUNT NO. 413

Date	Explanation	P.R.	DEBIT	CREDIT	BALANCE

Sales Discounts   ACCOUNT NO. 415

Date	Explanation	P.R.	DEBIT	CREDIT	BALANCE

Purchases   ACCOUNT NO. 505

Date	Explanation	P.R.	DEBIT	CREDIT	BALANCE

Purchases Returns and Allowances   ACCOUNT NO. 506

Date	Explanation	P.R.	DEBIT	CREDIT	BALANCE

Purchases Discount   ACCOUNT NO. 507

Date	Explanation	P.R.	DEBIT	CREDIT	BALANCE

Sales Salaries Expense   ACCOUNT NO. 621

Date	Explanation	P.R.	DEBIT	CREDIT	BALANCE

ACCOUNTS RECEIVABLE LEDGER

Date	Explanation	P.R.	DEBIT	CREDIT	BALANCE

Date	Explanation	P.R.	DEBIT	CREDIT	BALANCE

Date	Explanation	P.R.	DEBIT	CREDIT	BALANCE

ACCOUNTS PAYABLE LEDGER

Date	Explanation	P.R.	DEBIT	CREDIT	BALANCE

Date	Explanation	P.R.	DEBIT	CREDIT	BALANCE

Date	Explanation	P.R.	DEBIT	CREDIT	BALANCE

Date	Explanation	P.R.	DEBIT	CREDIT	BALANCE

Trial Balance

Schedule of Accounts Receivable

Schedule of Accounts Payable

Sales Journal — Page 2

Date	Account Debited	Invoice Number	PR	Accts. Rec. Dr. Sales Cr.	Cost of Goods Sold Dr. Inventory Cr.

Cash Receipts Journal — Page 2

Date	Account Credited	Explanation	PR	Cash Dr.	Sales Disc. Dr.	Accts. Rec. Cr.	Sales Cr.	Other Accts. Cr.	Cost of Goods Sold Dr. Inv. Cr.

Purchases Journal — Page 2

Date	Account	Date of Inv.	Terms	PR	Accts. Pay. Cr.	Inventory Dr.	Computer Supplies Dr.	Other Accts. Dr.

					Cash Disbursements Journal				Page 2
Date	Ck. No.	Payee	Account Debited	PR	Cash Cr.	Inventory Cr.	Other Accts. Dr.	Accts. Payable Dr.	

		GENERAL JOURNAL			Page 2
Date		**Account Titles and Explanation**	**P. R.**	**Debit**	**Credit**

Sales Journal					Page 2
Date	Account Debited	Invoice Number	PR	Accts. Rec. Dr. Sales Cr.	Cost of Goods Sold Dr. Inventory Cr.

Cash Receipts Journal								Page 2
Date	Account Credited	Explanation	PR	Cash Dr.	Sales Disc. Dr.	Accts. Rec. Cr.	Sales Cr.	Other Accts. Cr.	Cost of Goods Sold Dr. Inv. Cr.

Purchases Journal							Page 2
Date	Account	Date of Inv.	Terms	PR	Accts. Pay. Cr.	Inventory Dr.	Office Supplies Dr.	Other Accts. Dr.

					Cash Disbursements Journal				Page 2
Date	Ck. No.	Payee	Account Debited	PR	Cash Cr.	Inventory Cr.	Other Accts. Dr.	Accts. Payable Dr.	

	GENERAL JOURNAL			Page 3
Date	Account Titles and Explanation	P. R.	Debit	Credit
	Adjusting Entries			

	GENERAL JOURNAL			Page 3
Date	Account Titles and Explanation	P. R.	Debit	Credit
	Closing Entries			

| | | | | | GENERAL LEDGER | | | | |

Cash ACCOUNT NO. 101

Date	Explanation	P.R.	DEBIT	CREDIT	BALANCE
Apr. 30	Balance	√			50,247

Accounts Receivable ACCOUNT NO. 106

Date	Explanation	P.R.	DEBIT	CREDIT	BALANCE
Apr. 30	Balance	√			4,725

Merchandise Inventory ACCOUNT NO. 119

Date	Explanation	P.R.	DEBIT	CREDIT	BALANCE
Apr. 30	Balance	√			220,080

Office Supplies ACCOUNT NO. 124

Date	Explanation	P.R.	DEBIT	CREDIT	BALANCE
Apr. 30	Balance	√			430

Store Supplies   ACCOUNT NO. 125

Date	Explanation	P.R.	DEBIT	CREDIT	BALANCE
Apr. 30	Balance	√			2,447

Prepaid Insurance   ACCOUNT NO. 128

Date	Explanation	P.R.	DEBIT	CREDIT	BALANCE
Apr. 30	Balance	√			3,318

Office Equipment   ACCOUNT NO. 163

Date	Explanation	P.R.	DEBIT	CREDIT	BALANCE
Apr. 30	Balance	√			22,470

Accumulated Depreciation-Office Equipment   ACCOUNT NO. 164

Date	Explanation	P.R.	DEBIT	CREDIT	BALANCE
Apr. 30	Balance	√			9,898

Store Equipment   ACCOUNT NO. 165

Date	Explanation	P.R.	DEBIT	CREDIT	BALANCE
Apr. 30	Balance	√			38,920

Accumulated Depreciation-Store Equipment   ACCOUNT NO. 166

Date	Explanation	P.R.	DEBIT	CREDIT	BALANCE
Apr. 30	Balance	√			17,556

Accounts Payable — ACCOUNT NO. 201

Date	Explanation	P.R.	DEBIT	CREDIT	BALANCE
Apr. 30	Balance	√			7,098

Jenny Colo, Capital — ACCOUNT NO. 301

Date	Explanation	P.R.	DEBIT	CREDIT	BALANCE
Apr. 30	Balance	√			308,085

Jenny Colo, Withdrawals — ACCOUNT NO. 302

Date	Explanation	P.R.	DEBIT	CREDIT	BALANCE

Sales — ACCOUNT NO. 413

Date	Explanation	P.R.	DEBIT	CREDIT	BALANCE

Sales Returns and Allowances — ACCOUNT NO. 414

Date	Explanation	P.R.	DEBIT	CREDIT	BALANCE

Sales Discounts   ACCOUNT NO. 415

Date	Explanation	P.R.	DEBIT	CREDIT	BALANCE

Cost of Goods Sold   ACCOUNT NO. 502

Date	Explanation	P.R.	DEBIT	CREDIT	BALANCE

Depreciation Expense-Office Equipment   ACCOUNT NO. 612

Date	Explanation	P.R.	DEBIT	CREDIT	BALANCE

Depreciation Expense-Store Equipment   ACCOUNT NO. 613

Date	Explanation	P.R.	DEBIT	CREDIT	BALANCE

Office Salaries Expense   ACCOUNT NO. 620

Date	Explanation	P.R.	DEBIT	CREDIT	BALANCE

Sales Salaries Expense   ACCOUNT NO. 621

Date	Explanation	P.R.	DEBIT	CREDIT	BALANCE

Insurance Expense — ACCOUNT NO. 637

Date	Explanation	P.R.	DEBIT	CREDIT	BALANCE

Rent Expense-Office Space — ACCOUNT NO. 641

Date	Explanation	P.R.	DEBIT	CREDIT	BALANCE

Rent Expense-Selling Space — ACCOUNT NO. 642

Date	Explanation	P.R.	DEBIT	CREDIT	BALANCE

Office Supplies Expense — ACCOUNT NO. 650

Date	Explanation	P.R.	DEBIT	CREDIT	BALANCE

Store Supplies Expense — ACCOUNT NO. 651

Date	Explanation	P.R.	DEBIT	CREDIT	BALANCE

Utilities Expense — ACCOUNT NO. 690

Date	Explanation	P.R.	DEBIT	CREDIT	BALANCE

	Income Summary			ACCOUNT NO. 901	
Date	Explanation	P.R.	DEBIT	CREDIT	BALANCE

ACCOUNTS RECEIVABLE LEDGER

NAME   Crane Corp.

Date	Explanation	P.R.	DEBIT	CREDIT	BALANCE

NAME   Hensel Company

Date	Explanation	P.R.	DEBIT	CREDIT	BALANCE

NAME   Knox, Inc.

Date	Explanation	P.R.	DEBIT	CREDIT	BALANCE
Apr. 28		S2	4,725		4,725

NAME   Lee Services

Date	Explanation	P.R.	DEBIT	CREDIT	BALANCE

ACCOUNTS PAYABLE LEDGER					

NAME   Fink Corp.

Date	Explanation	P.R.	DEBIT	CREDIT	BALANCE

NAME   Garcia Inc.

Date	Explanation	P.R.	DEBIT	CREDIT	BALANCE

NAME   Peyton Products

Date	Explanation	P.R.	DEBIT	CREDIT	BALANCE
Apr. 29		P2		7,098	7,098

NAME   Gear Supply Co.

Date	Explanation	P.R.	DEBIT	CREDIT	BALANCE

Chapter 7 Comprehensive Problem

Name _____

Colo Company (Continued)

Colo Company
Work Sheet
For Month Ended May 31, 2005

Account Titles	Unadjusted Trial Balance		Adjustments		Adjusted Trial Balance		Income Statement		Balance Sheet & Statement of Owner's Equity	
	Dr.	Cr.	Dr.	Cr.	Dr.	Cr.	Dr.	Cr.	Dr.	Cr.

Colo Company
Income Statement
For Month Ended May 31, 2005

Colo Company
Statement of Owner's Equity
For Month Ended May 31, 2005

Colo Company
Balance Sheet
May 31, 2005

Colo Company
Post-Closing Trial Balance
May 31, 2005

Colo Company
Schedule of Accounts Receivable
May 31, 2005

Colo Company
Schedule of Accounts Payable
May 31, 2005

(1) _____

_____

(2) _____

_____

_____

_____

_____

_____

_____

_____

_____

_____

_____

_____

(3) Roll On: _____

_____

_____

_____

_____

_____

_____

Segment	% Change	Current	% Change	One Year Prior	Two Years Prior

(1) Part 1 Interpretation: _____

_____

_____

_____

_____

(2) Part 2 Interpretation: _____

_____

_____

_____

_____

(1) _____
_____
_____
_____
_____
_____
_____

(2) _____
_____
_____
_____
_____
_____
_____
_____
_____
_____

(3) _____
_____
_____
_____
_____
_____
_____
_____
_____
_____
_____
_____
_____

MEMORANDUM

TO:
FROM:
SUBJECT:
DATE:

(1) _____

_____

_____

_____

(2) _____

_____

_____

_____

_____

_____

(3) _____

_____

_____

_____

_____

_____

_____

_____

_____

_____

_____

(4) _____

_____

_____

_____

_____

_____

_____

_____

_____

_____

_____

SALES JOURNAL					Page 2
Date	Account Debited	Invoice Number	PR	Accts. Rec. Dr. Sales Cr.	Cost of Goods Sold Dr. Inventory Cr.

Cash Receipts Journal								
Date	Account Credited	Explanation	PR	Cash Dr.	Sales Disc. Dr.	Accts. Rec. Cr.	Sales Cr.	Other Accts. Cr.	Cost of Goods Sold Dr. Inv. Cr.

						Purchases Journal			Page 2
Date	Account	Date of Invoice	Terms	PR	Accts. Payable Cr.	Inventory Dr.	Office Supplies Dr.	Other Accts. Dr.	

					Cash Disbursements Journal				Page 2
Date	Ck. No.	Payee	Account Debited	PR	Cash Cr.	Inventory Cr.	Other Accts. Dr.	Accts. Payable Dr.	

GENERAL JOURNAL   Page 2

Date	Account Titles and Explanation	P.R.	Debit	Credit

GENERAL LEDGER

Cash   ACCOUNT NO. 101

Date	Explanation	P.R.	DEBIT	CREDIT	BALANCE

Accounts Receivable   ACCOUNT NO. 106

Date	Explanation	P.R.	DEBIT	CREDIT	BALANCE

Inventory   ACCOUNT NO. 119

Date	Explanation	P.R.	DEBIT	CREDIT	BALANCE

Office Supplies   ACCOUNT NO. 124

Date	Explanation	P.R.	DEBIT	CREDIT	BALANCE

Store Supplies   ACCOUNT NO. 125

Date	Explanation	P.R.	DEBIT	CREDIT	BALANCE

Office Equipment   ACCOUNT NO. 163

Date	Explanation	P.R.	DEBIT	CREDIT	BALANCE

Accounts Payable — ACCOUNT NO. 201

Date	Explanation	P.R.	DEBIT	CREDIT	BALANCE

Long-Term Notes Payable — ACCOUNT NO. 251

Date	Explanation	P.R.	DEBIT	CREDIT	BALANCE

, Capital — ACCOUNT NO. 308

Date	Explanation	P.R.	DEBIT	CREDIT	BALANCE

Sales — ACCOUNT NO. 413

Date	Explanation	P.R.	DEBIT	CREDIT	BALANCE

Sales Discounts — ACCOUNT NO. 415

Date	Explanation	P.R.	DEBIT	CREDIT	BALANCE

Cost of Goods Sold — ACCOUNT NO. 502

Date	Explanation	P.R.	DEBIT	CREDIT	BALANCE

Sales Salaries Expense   ACCOUNT NO. 621

Date	Explanation	P.R.	DEBIT	CREDIT	BALANCE

ACCOUNTS RECEIVABLE LEDGER

Date	Explanation	P.R.	DEBIT	CREDIT	BALANCE

Date	Explanation	P.R.	DEBIT	CREDIT	BALANCE

Date	Explanation	P.R.	DEBIT	CREDIT	BALANCE

ACCOUNTS PAYABLE LEDGER

Date	Explanation	P.R.	DEBIT	CREDIT	BALANCE

Date	Explanation	P.R.	DEBIT	CREDIT	BALANCE

Date	Explanation	P.R.	DEBIT	CREDIT	BALANCE

Date	Explanation	P.R.	DEBIT	CREDIT	BALANCE

Trial Balance

Schedule of Accounts Receivable

Schedule of Accounts Payable

Name _____

(1) _____
_____
_____
_____
_____
_____
_____

(2) _____
_____
_____
_____
_____
_____
_____

(3) _____
_____
_____
_____
_____
_____

(4) _____
_____
_____
_____
_____

Name _____

(1) _____
_____
_____
_____

(2) _____
_____
_____
_____
_____
_____
_____
_____
_____
_____
_____
_____
_____
_____
_____
_____
_____
_____
_____
_____
_____

(3) _____
_____
_____
_____
_____
_____
_____

(1) _____

_____

_____

(2) _____

_____

_____

(3) _____

_____

_____

(4) _____

_____

_____

(1) _____

_____

_____

_____

_____

_____

(2) _____

_____

_____

_____

_____

(3) _____

_____

_____

_____

_____

Quick Study 8-2

(1) (a) _____

_____

   (b) _____

   (c) _____

(2) _____

_____

Quick Study 8-3

(1) _____

_____

_____

_____

_____

(2) _____

_____

_____

_____

(1) _____
_____
_____

(2) _____
_____
_____

(3) _____
_____
_____

Quick Study 8-5

(1)

GENERAL JOURNAL

Date	Account Titles and Explanation	P. R.	Debit	Credit
(a) Establishment of the Fund:				
(b) Reimbursement of the Fund at Month-End:				

(2) _____
_____
_____

Parts 1 and 2

	(1)		(2)
	Bank or Book Effect	**Add or Subtract**	**Journal Entry Required or Not**
(a)			
(b)			
(c)			
(d)			
(e)			
(f)			
(g)			

Quick Study 8-7

Days' Sales Uncollected (2005): _____

_____
_____
_____
_____

Days' Sales Uncollected (2004): _____

_____
_____
_____
_____

Interpretation and Explanation: _____

_____
_____
_____
_____

Quick Study 8-8

(a) _____

_____

(b) _____

_____
_____
_____

(1) _____

_____

_____

_____

_____

(2) _____

_____

_____

_____

_____

_____

Exercise 8-2

(a) Internal Control Problems: _____

_____

_____

_____

_____

_____

_____

(b) Internal Control Recommendations: _____

_____

_____

_____

_____

Exercise 8-3

Evaluation: _____

_____

_____

_____

Principles Ignored: _____

_____

_____

_____

_____

(1) Establish the Fund

GENERAL JOURNAL

Date	Account Titles and Explanation	P. R.	Debit	Credit

(2) Reimburse and Reduce the Fund

GENERAL JOURNAL

Date	Account Titles and Explanation	P.R.	Debit	Credit

(1) Establish the Fund

GENERAL JOURNAL

Date		Account Titles and Explanation	P. R.	Debit	Credit

(2) Reimburse the Fund

GENERAL JOURNAL

Date		Account Titles and Explanation	P. R.	Debit	Credit

(3) Reimburse and Increase the Fund

GENERAL JOURNAL

Date		Account Titles and Explanation	P. R.	Debit	Credit

Name _____

	Bank Balance		Book Balance			Not Shown on the Reconciliation
	Add	Deduct	Add	Deduct	Adjust	
1. Bank service charge.						
2. Checks written and mailed to payees on October 2.						
3. Check written by another depositor but charged against the company's account.						
4. Principle and interest collected by the bank but not recorded by the company.						
5. Special charge for collection of note in part 4 on company's behalf.						
6. Check written against the company account and cleared by the bank; erroneously omitted by the company's recordkeeper.						
7. Interest earned on the account.						
8. Deposit made on September 30 after the bank closed.						
9. Checks outstanding on August 31 that cleared the bank in September.						
10. NSF check from customer returned on September 25 but not recorded by the company						
11. Checks written and mailed to payees on September 30.						
12. Deposit made on September 5 and processed on September 8.						

Chapter 8   Exercise 8-7   *Name* _____

(1) _____
_____
_____

(2) _____
_____

(3) _____
_____

Exercise 8-8

_____
_____

Bank Reconciliation

_____
_____
_____
_____
_____
_____
_____
_____
_____
_____
_____
_____

Exercise 8-9

GENERAL JOURNAL

Date	Account Titles and Explanation	P. R.	Debit	Credit

Name _____

Days' Sales Uncollected (2004): _____
_____
_____
_____

Days' Sales Uncollected (2005): _____
_____
_____
_____

Interpretation of Change: _____
_____
_____
_____
_____

(a) Recording Invoices at Gross Amounts--Gross Method

GENERAL JOURNAL

Date	Account Titles and Explanation	P. R.	Debit	Credit

(a) Recording Invoices at Net Amounts--Net Method

GENERAL JOURNAL

Date	Account Titles and Explanation	P. R.	Debit	Credit

(1) **Principle Violated:**

    Recommended

(2) **Principle Violated:**

    Recommended

(3) **Principle Violated:**

    Recommended

(4) **Principle Violated:**

    Recommended

(5) **Principle Violated:**

    Recommended

GENERAL JOURNAL

Date	Account Titles and Explanation	P. R.	Debit	Credit

Part 2

_____
_____
_____
_____
_____
_____
_____
_____
_____
_____

Part 1

GENERAL JOURNAL

Date		Account Titles and Explanation	P. R.	Debit	Credit

Part 2

_____

Petty Cash Payments Report

_____
_____
_____
_____
_____
_____
_____
_____
_____
_____
_____
_____
_____
_____
_____
_____
_____
_____

Part 3

GENERAL JOURNAL

Date		Account Titles and Explanation	P.R.	Debit	Credit

Bank Reconciliation

Part 2

GENERAL JOURNAL

Date	Account Titles and Explanation	P. R.	Debit	Credit

(a) _____

_____

_____

_____

_____

_____

_____

(b) _____

_____

_____

_____

_____

_____

_____

Problem 8-5A or 8-5B
Part 1

_____

_____

Bank Reconciliation

_____

_____

_____

_____

_____

_____

_____

_____

_____

_____

_____

_____

_____

_____

GENERAL JOURNAL

Date	Account Titles and Explanation	P. R.	Debit	Credit

Part 3

(1) _____

_____

(2) _____

_____

(3) _____

_____

_____
_____

Bank Reconciliation

_____
==
_____
_____
_____
_____
_____
_____
_____
_____
_____
_____
_____
_____
_____
_____
_____
_____
_____
_____

Part 2

GENERAL JOURNAL

Date		Account Titles and Explanation	P. R.	Debit	Credit

Part 1

Item	Feb. 2, 2003		Feb. 3, 2002	
	Balance ($)	Cash & Equiv. as % of Balance	Balance ($)	Cash & Equiv. as % of Balance

Interpretation: _____

_____

_____

_____

Part 2

Days' Sales Uncollected (Feb. 2, 2003): _____

_____

_____

_____

_____

_____

Days' Sales Uncollected (Feb. 3, 2002): _____

_____

_____

_____

_____

_____

Interpretation: _____

_____

_____

_____

_____

_____

Part 4

Roll On: _____

_____

_____

_____

_____

_____

_____

_____

_____

_____

_____

Krispy Kreme:
Days' Sales Uncollected (Current year): _____
_____
_____

Days' Sales Uncollected (Prior year): _____
_____
_____

Interpretation: _____
_____
_____
_____

Tastykake:
Days' Sales Uncollected (Current year): _____
_____
_____

Days' Sales Uncollected (Prior year): _____
_____
_____

Interpretation: _____
_____
_____

Comparison - Krisky Kreme vs. Tastykake: _____
_____
_____
_____

(1) _____

_____

_____

_____

_____

(2) _____

_____

_____

_____

_____

(3) _____

_____

_____

_____

_____

_____

_____

_____

(4) _____

_____

_____

_____

_____

_____

_____

_____

MEMORANDUM

TO:

FROM:

SUBJECT:

DATE:

(1) _____

_____

(2) _____

_____

(3) _____

_____

(4) _____

_____

(5) _____

_____

(6) _____

_____

(7) _____

_____

(8) _____

_____

(9) _____

_____

(10) _____

_____

(11) _____

_____

(12) _____

_____

_____

(1) _____

_____

(2) _____

_____

(3) _____

_____

(4) _____

_____

(5) _____

_____

(6) _____

_____

(7) _____

_____

(8) _____

_____

(9) _____

_____

(10) _____

_____

(11) _____

_____

(1) _____

_____

_____

(2) _____

_____

_____

(3) _____

_____

_____

_____

(4) _____

_____

_____

_____

_____

_____

(5) _____

_____

_____

_____

(1) _____
_____
_____

(2) _____
_____
_____

(3) _____
_____
_____

(4) _____
_____
_____

(5) _____
_____
_____

(6) _____
_____
_____

(7) _____
_____
_____

Hitting the Road--BTN 8-9

_____
_____
_____
_____
_____
_____
_____
_____

1. _____

_____

_____

2. _____

_____

_____

3. _____

_____

_____

4. _____

_____

_____

5. _____

_____

_____

6. _____

_____

_____

(1)

GENERAL JOURNAL

Date		Account Titles and Explanation	P. R.	Debit	Credit

(2)

GENERAL JOURNAL

Date		Account Titles and Explanation	P. R.	Debit	Credit

(1)

GENERAL JOURNAL

Date		Account Titles and Explanation	P. R.	Debit	Credit

(2)

GENERAL JOURNAL

Date		Account Titles and Explanation	P. R.	Debit	Credit

(1)

GENERAL JOURNAL

Date		Account Titles and Explanation	P. R.	Debit	Credit

(2) _____

_____

_____

(3)

GENERAL JOURNAL

Date		Account Titles and Explanation	P. R.	Debit	Credit

Quick Study 9-4

GENERAL JOURNAL

Date		Account Titles and Explanation	P. R.	Debit	Credit

GENERAL JOURNAL

Date	Account Titles and Explanation	P. R.	Debit	Credit

Quick Study 9-6

Accounts Receivable Turnover: _____
_____
_____
_____

Interpretation: _____
_____
_____
_____

GENERAL JOURNAL

Date	Account Titles and Explanation	P. R.	Debit	Credit

GENERAL LEDGER

Accounts Receivable	Sales	Sales Returns and Allowances

ACCOUNTS RECEIVABLE LEDGER

Surf Shop	Yum Enterprises	Matt Albin

Part 2

Schedule of Accounts Receivable

Comparison:

GENERAL JOURNAL

Date		Account Titles and Explanation	P. R.	Debit	Credit

(a)

GENERAL JOURNAL

Date	Account Titles and Explanation	P. R.	Debit	Credit

(b)

GENERAL JOURNAL

Date	Account Titles and Explanation	P. R.	Debit	Credit

GENERAL JOURNAL

Date	Account Titles and Explanation	P. R.	Debit	Credit

Financial Statement Note(s): _____

_____

_____

_____

GENERAL JOURNAL

Date	Account Titles and Explanation	P. R.	Debit	Credit

GENERAL JOURNAL

Date	Account Titles and Explanation	P. R.	Debit	Credit

GENERAL JOURNAL

Date	Account Titles and Explanation	P. R.	Debit	Credit

Accounts Receivable Turnover (2004): _____

_____

_____

Accounts Receivable Turnover (2005): _____

_____

_____

Comparison and Interpretation: _____

_____

_____

Name _____

GENERAL JOURNAL

Date	Account Titles and Explanation	P. R.	Debit	Credit

2004

GENERAL JOURNAL

Date		Account Titles and Explanation	P. R.	Debit	Credit

Supporting work:

2005

GENERAL JOURNAL

Date	Account Titles and Explanation	P. R.	Debit	Credit

Supporting work:

GENERAL JOURNAL

Date		Account Titles and Explanation	P. R.	Debit	Credit
(a)					
(b)					
(c)					

Part 2

_____
_____
_____
_____
_____
_____
_____
_____

==

_____

_____

_____

_____

_____

_____

_____

Problem 9-4A or 9-4B
Part 1

_____

_____

_____

_____

_____

_____

_____

_____

_____

Part 2

GENERAL JOURNAL

Date	Account Titles and Explanation	P. R.	Debit	Credit

Part 3

_____

_____

_____

_____

_____

_____

_____

_____

Date	Account Titles and Explanation	P. R.	Debit	Credit
2004				
2005				

Date	Account Titles and Explanation	P. R.	Debit	Credit

Part 2

Reporting: _____

_____

_____

Reasoning: _____

_____

_____

Principle: _____

_____

_____

_____

Name _____

GENERAL JOURNAL

Date		Account Titles and Explanation	P. R.	Debit	Credit
(a)					
(b)					

Part 2

_____
_____
_____
_____
_____
_____

GENERAL JOURNAL

Date		Account Titles and Explanation	P. R.	Debit	Credit

Part 3

_____
_____
_____
_____
_____
_____
_____

(1) _____

_____

(2) Liquid Assets as a percent of Current Liabilities (Feb. 2, 2003):

_____

_____

_____

Liquid Assets as a percent of Current Liabilities (Feb. 3, 2002):

_____

_____

_____

Comparison and Interpretation:

_____

_____

_____

_____

_____

(3) _____

_____

_____

_____

(4) Accounts Receivable Turnover (2003):

_____

_____

(5) Roll On:

_____

_____

_____

_____

_____

_____

_____

_____

_____

Name _____

(1) Krispy Kreme's Accounts Receivable Turnover (Current Year and Prior Year):

_____
_____
_____
_____

Tastykake's Accounts Receivable Turnover (Current Year and Prior Year):

_____
_____
_____
_____

(2) Krispy Kreme's Average Collection Period (Current Year and Prior Year):

_____
_____
_____

Tastykake's Average Collection Period (Current Year and Prior Year):

_____
_____
_____

(3) Efficiency Comparison:

_____
_____
_____

(4) Krispy Kreme's Percent of Uncollectibles (Current Year and Prior Year)

_____
_____
_____

Tastykake's Percent of Uncollectibles (Current Year and Prior Year)

_____
_____
_____

Comparison:

_____
_____
_____

(1) _____
_____
_____
_____
_____
_____
_____
_____

(2) _____
_____
_____
_____
_____
_____
_____
_____
_____
_____
_____
_____

(3) _____
_____
_____
_____
_____
_____
_____
_____
_____

MEMORANDUM

TO:

FROM:

SUBJECT:

DATE:

(1) _____

_____

_____

_____

_____

_____

(2) _____

_____

_____

_____

_____

_____

Estimate of Uncollectibles: _____

_____

_____

_____

_____

_____

_____

Adjusting Entry:

GENERAL JOURNAL

Date	Account Titles and Explanation	P. R.	Debit	Credit

Presentation of Net Realizable Accounts Receivable in Balance Sheet:

_____

_____

_____

_____

_____

(1) _____
_____
_____
_____

(2) _____
_____

(3) _____
_____
_____

(4) _____
_____
_____
_____
_____

Added Monthly Net Income (Loss) under Plan A

Added Monthly Net Income (Loss) under Plan B

Part 2

_____
_____
_____
_____
_____
_____
_____
_____
_____
_____
_____
_____
_____
_____
_____
_____
_____
_____
_____
_____

Global Decision--BTN 9-10

(1) _____
_____
_____
_____
_____
_____

(2) _____
_____
_____
_____
_____
_____
_____

Name _____

_____

_____

_____

_____

_____

_____

Quick Study 10-2

(1) _____

_____

_____

(2) _____

_____

_____

(3) _____

_____

_____

Quick Study 10-3

(1) Straight-line: _____

_____

(2) Units-of-Production: _____

_____

_____

_____

Quick Study 10-4

Revised Straight-Line Depreciation: _____

_____

_____

_____

_____

First Year: _____

_____

Second Year: _____

_____

Third Year: _____

_____

Quick Study 10-6

(1)

    (a) _____

    (b) _____

    (c) _____

    (d) _____

(2)

GENERAL JOURNAL

Date	Account Titles and Explanation	P. R.	Debit	Credit
(a)				
(b)				

Name _____

GENERAL JOURNAL

Date	Account Titles and Explanation	P. R.	Debit	Credit
(1)				
(2)				

Quick Study 10-8

GENERAL JOURNAL

Date	Account Titles and Explanation	P. R.	Debit	Credit
(1)				
(2)				

Intangible Assets(s): _____
_____

Natural Resources(s): _____
_____

Quick Study 10-10

GENERAL JOURNAL

Date		Account Titles and Explanation	P. R.	Debit	Credit
(1)					
(2)					

Quick Study 10-11

Total Asset Turnover: _____
_____
_____

Interpretation: _____
_____
_____

Chapter 10   Exercise 10-1   Name _____

Total Cost to be Recorded: _____
_____
_____
_____
_____
_____
_____
_____

Exercise 10-2

Cost of Assets: _____
_____
_____
_____
_____
_____
_____
_____

GENERAL JOURNAL

Date	Account Titles and Explanation	P. R.	Debit	Credit

Allocation of Costs to Assets:

_____
_____
_____
_____
_____
_____
_____
_____
_____
_____
_____

GENERAL JOURNAL

Date	Account Titles and Explanation	P. R.	Debit	Credit

Name _____

(1) Straight-Line Depreciation:

Year	Annual Depreciation	Year-End Book Value

(2) Double-Declining-Balance Depreciation:

Year	Beginning-Year Book Value	Depreciation Rate	Annual Depreciation	Year-End Book Value

Name _____

(1) Straight-Line: _____
_____
_____
_____

(2) Units-of-Production: _____
_____
_____
_____
_____
_____

(3) Double-Declining-Balance: _____
_____
_____
_____
_____
_____

Exercise 10-6

(1) Straight-Line: _____
_____
_____
_____

(2) Double-Declining-Balance: _____
_____
_____
_____
_____
_____
_____

(1) _____

_____

_____

_____

_____

(2) _____

_____

_____

_____

_____

_____

_____

_____

Name _____

(1) Straight-Line Depreciation:

Year	Income before Depreciation	Depreciation Expense	Net Income

(2) Double-Declining-Balance Depreciation:

Year	Income before Depreciation	Depreciation Expense	Net Income

(1) _____

_____

_____

_____

_____

(2)

GENERAL JOURNAL

Date		Account Titles and Explanation	P. R.	Debit	Credit

(3) _____

_____

_____

_____

_____

_____

(4)

GENERAL JOURNAL

Date		Account Titles and Explanation	P. R.	Debit	Credit

Name _____

GENERAL JOURNAL

Date	Account Titles and Explanation	P. R.	Debit	Credit
(1)				
(2)				
(3)				

Exercise 10-11

(1) _____

_____

_____

(2) _____

_____

_____

(3) _____

_____

_____

Name _____

GENERAL JOURNAL

Date	Account Titles and Explanation	P. R.	Debit	Credit
(1)				
(2)				
(3)				

GENERAL JOURNAL

Date	Account Titles and Explanation	P. R.	Debit	Credit
(1)				
(2)				

Computations:

Exercise 10-14

GENERAL JOURNAL

Date	Account Titles and Explanation	P. R.	Debit	Credit

Name _____

GENERAL JOURNAL

Date	Account Titles and Explanation	P. R.	Debit	Credit

Exercise 10-16

(1) Value of Goodwill: _____

_____

_____

_____

_____

(2) Value of Goodwill: _____

_____

_____

_____

_____

Exercise 10-17

(1) _____

_____

(2) _____

_____

(3) _____

_____

Name _____

Total Asset Turnover (2004): _____

_____

_____

Total Asset Turnover (2005): _____

_____

_____

Efficiency Analysis: _____

_____

_____

_____

_____

Name _____

	Appraised Value	Percent of Total	Apportioned Cost
Building.............................			
Land..................................			
Land Improvments..............			
Vehicles (or Trucks)............	_____	_____	
Total.................................	_____	_____	

GENERAL JOURNAL

Date	Account Titles and Explanation	P. R.	Debit	Credit

Part 2

_____
_____
_____
_____

Part 3

_____
_____
_____
_____
_____
_____

Part 4

_____
_____
_____
_____
_____
_____
_____

Chapter 10   Problem 10-2A or 10-2B   Name _____
Part 1   (Continued)

	Land	Building 2 (or B)	Building 3 (or C)	Land Improv. 1 (or B)	Land Improv. 2 (or C)
Purchase price.........					
Demolition..............					
Land grading...........					
New building...........					
New improvements...					
Totals....................					

Computations:

GENERAL JOURNAL

Date		Account Titles and Explanation	P. R.	Debit	Credit

Part 3

GENERAL JOURNAL

Date		Account Titles and Explanation	P. R.	Debit	Credit

2004:

GENERAL JOURNAL

Date		Account Titles and Explanation	P. R.	Debit	Credit

Supporting work:

2005:

GENERAL JOURNAL

Date	Account Titles and Explanation	P. R.	Debit	Credit

Supporting work:

2004:

GENERAL JOURNAL

Date		Account Titles and Explanation	P. R.	Debit	Credit

2005:

GENERAL JOURNAL

Date		Account Titles and Explanation	P. R.	Debit	Credit

Supporting work:

2006:

GENERAL JOURNAL

Date	Account Titles and Explanation	P. R.	Debit	Credit

Supporting work:

Part 1

Year	Straight-Line	Units-of-Production	Double-Declining-Balance
1			
2			
3			
4			
5 (for 10-5B)	_____	_____	_____
Totals	_____	_____	_____

Workspace:

Straight-Line: _____

_____

_____

Units-of-Production: _____

_____

_____

_____

_____

Double-Declining-Balance: _____

_____

_____

_____

_____

Part 2

(a)

GENERAL JOURNAL

Date	Account Titles and Explanation	P. R.	Debit	Credit

(b)

GENERAL JOURNAL

Date	Account Titles and Explanation	P. R.	Debit	Credit

(c)

GENERAL JOURNAL

Date	Account Titles and Explanation	P. R.	Debit	Credit
(i) Sold for $_____ cash:				
(ii) Sold for $_____ cash:				
(iii) Destroyed in fire, collected $_____ cash from insurance.				

GENERAL JOURNAL

Date	Account Titles and Explanation	P. R.	Debit	Credit
(a)				
(b)				
(c)				
(d)				
(e)				
(f)				

GENERAL JOURNAL

Date	Account Titles and Explanation	P. R.	Debit	Credit

Analysis Component:

_____

_____

_____

_____

_____

_____

_____

_____

Name _____

Part 1

_____

_____

_____

_____

_____

_____

Part 2

_____

_____

_____

_____

_____

_____

Part 3

_____

_____

_____

_____

_____

Part 4

_____

_____

_____

_____

_____

_____

_____

_____

(1) _____

_____

_____

_____

_____

_____

(2)	December 31, 2004	December 31, 2005
Office Equipment:		
Computer Equipment:		
(3) Total Asset Turnover:		
Analysis:		

Name _____

(1) As of Feb. 2, 2003: _____
_____
_____

As of Feb. 3, 2002 _____
_____
_____
_____
_____

(2) _____
_____
_____
_____

(3) _____
_____
_____
_____
_____
_____
_____

(4) Total Asset Turnover (2003): _____
_____
_____
_____

Total Asset Turnover (2002): _____
_____
_____
_____

(5) Roll On: _____
_____
_____
_____
_____

Name _____

(1) Total Asset Turnover (Krispy Kreme): _____

       Current Year

_____

_____

       One Year Prior

_____

_____

  Total Asset Turnover (Tastykake):

       Current Year

_____

_____

       One Year Prior

_____

_____

(2) Efficiency Analysis:

_____

_____

_____

_____

_____

(1) _____
_____
_____
_____
_____
_____
_____
_____

(2) _____
_____
_____
_____
_____
_____
_____
_____
_____
_____
_____

(3) _____
_____
_____
_____
_____
_____
_____
_____
_____
_____

DATA FOR MEMORANDUM						
Total Asset Turnover	Company 1	Company 2	Company 3	Company 4	Company 5	Average

MEMORANDUM

TO:
FROM:
SUBJECT:
DATE:

(1) _____
_____
_____
_____

(2) _____
_____
_____
_____
_____
_____
_____

(3) _____
_____
_____
_____
_____

| Presentation Outline |

Method of Expertise: _____

_____
_____
_____
_____
_____

Depreciation Expense: _____

_____
_____
_____
_____
_____
_____

Explanations: _____

_____
_____
_____
_____
_____
_____

Analysis Versus Other Methods: _____

_____
_____
_____
_____
_____

Book Value and Reporting: _____

_____
_____
_____
_____
_____

(1) _____
_____
_____
_____
_____

(2) _____
_____

(3) _____
_____
_____
_____
_____
_____

(4) _____
_____
_____
_____
_____

(a) _____
_____
_____
_____
_____
_____
_____
_____
_____

(b) _____
_____
_____
_____
_____
_____
_____
_____

Part 2

_____
_____
_____
_____
_____
_____
_____
_____

_____
_____
_____
_____
_____
_____
_____
_____
_____
_____
_____
_____
_____
_____
_____
_____
_____
_____
_____

Global Decision--BTN 10-10

(1) Total Asset Turnover (Current Year): _____
_____
_____

   Total Asset Turnover (Prior Year): _____
_____
_____

(2) _____
_____
_____
_____
_____
_____
_____

Current Liabilities: _____

_____

_____

Quick Study 11-2

GENERAL JOURNAL

Date		Account Titles and Explanation	P. R.	Debit	Credit

Quick Study 11-3

GENERAL JOURNAL

Date		Account Titles and Explanation	P. R.	Debit	Credit

(1) Accrued Interest Payable: _____

_____

_____

_____

(2) & (3)

GENERAL JOURNAL

Date	Account Titles and Explanation	P. R.	Debit	Credit

Quick Study 11-5

GENERAL JOURNAL

Date	Account Titles and Explanation	P. R.	Debit	Credit

Quick Study 11-6

GENERAL JOURNAL

Date	Account Titles and Explanation	P. R.	Debit	Credit

GENERAL JOURNAL

Date		Account Titles and Explanation	P. R.	Debit	Credit

Quick Study 11-8

(1) _____

(2) _____

(3) _____

Quick Study 11-9

Times Interest Earned: _____

_____

_____

Interpretation: _____

_____

_____

Quick Study 11-10^B

GENERAL JOURNAL

Date		Account Titles and Explanation	P. R.	Debit	Credit

(1)	_____	(6)	_____
(2)	_____	(7)	_____
(3)	_____	(8)	_____
(4)	_____	(9)	_____
(5)	_____	(10)	_____

Exercise 11-2

GENERAL JOURNAL

Date		Account Titles and Explanation	P. R.	Debit	Credit
(1)					
(2)					
(3)					
(4)					
(5)					
(6)					

1. _____

_____

_____

_____

2.

GENERAL JOURNAL

Date		Account Titles and Explanation	P. R.	Debit	Credit

3.

GENERAL JOURNAL

Date		Account Titles and Explanation	P. R.	Debit	Credit

Name _____

(1) Maturity Date: _____

_____

_____

(2)

GENERAL JOURNAL

Date	Account Titles and Explanation	P. R.	Debit	Credit

(1) Maturity Date: _____

_____

_____

_____

(2) Interest Expense (2005): _____

_____

_____

_____

_____

(3) Interest Expense (2006): _____

_____

_____

_____

_____

(4)

GENERAL JOURNAL

Date	Account Titles and Explanation	P. R.	Debit	Credit

Name _____

	Subject to Tax	Rate	Tax
(a)			
FICA-Social Security..........	_____	_____	_____
FICA-Medicare.................	_____	_____	_____
FUTA.............................	_____	_____	_____
SUTA.............................	_____	_____	_____
(b)			
FICA-Social Security..........	_____	_____	_____
FICA-Medicare.................	_____	_____	_____
FUTA.............................	_____	_____	_____
SUTA.............................	_____	_____	_____
(c)			
FICA-Social Security..........	_____	_____	_____
FICA-Medicare.................	_____	_____	_____
FUTA.............................	_____	_____	_____
SUTA.............................	_____	_____	_____

GENERAL JOURNAL

Date		Account Titles and Explanation	P. R.	Debit	Credit

Exercise 11-8

(1) _____

_____

(2) _____

_____

(3) _____

_____

(4) _____

_____

_____

_____

(5)

GENERAL JOURNAL

Date		Account Titles and Explanation	P. R.	Debit	Credit

Exercise 11-9

(a) _____

_____

(b) _____

_____

(c) _____

_____

(d) _____

_____

(e) _____

_____

(f) _____

_____

Analysis: _____

_____

_____

_____
_____
_____
_____
_____
_____
_____
_____
_____

Exercise 11-11^A

_____
_____
_____
_____
_____
_____
_____
_____
_____

Exercise 11-12^B

(1) _____
_____
_____
_____

(2)

GENERAL JOURNAL

Date	Account Titles and Explanation	P. R.	Debit	Credit

Chapter 11   Problem 11-1A or 11-1B   **Name** _____

(1) Maturity Dates: _____

_____

_____

_____

_____

_____

_____

_____

(2) Interest Due at Maturity: _____

_____

_____

_____

_____

_____

_____

_____

(3) Accrued Interest at the End of 2004: _____

_____

_____

_____

_____

_____

(4) Interest Expense in 2005: _____

_____

_____

_____

_____

_____

(5)

GENERAL JOURNAL

Date	Account Titles and Explanation	P. R.	Debit	Credit

(1)

GENERAL JOURNAL

Date	Account Titles and Explanation	P. R.	Debit	Credit
2004				

(1) (Continued from prior page)

GENERAL JOURNAL

Date	Account Titles and Explanation	P. R.	Debit	Credit
2005				

(2) Warranty Expense for November 2004 and December 2004: _____

_____

_____

_____

_____

_____

(3) Warranty Expense for January 2005: _____

_____

_____

_____

_____

(4) Balance of the Estimated Warranty Liability as of December 31, 2004: ___

_____

_____

_____

_____

(5) Balance of the Estimated Warranty Liability as of December 31, 2005: ___

_____

_____

_____

_____

_____

(1) _____ **Company:**

Times Interest Earned: _____

_____

_____

_____

_____

(2) _____ **Company:**

Times Interest Earned: _____

_____

_____

_____

_____

(3)   Sales Increase by _____ **%**

	_____ Company	_____ Company
Sales		
Variable expenses		
Income before interest		
Interest expense (fixed)		
Net Income		
Net income percent change		

(4)   Sales Increase by _____ **%**

	_____ Company	_____ Company
Sales		
Variable expenses		
Income before interest		
Interest expense (fixed)		
Net Income		
Net income percent change		

(5)   Sales Increase by _____ %

	_____ Company	_____ Company
Sales		
Variable expenses		
Income before interest		
Interest expense (fixed)		
Net Income		
Net income percent change		

(6)   Sales Decrease by _____ %

	_____ Company	_____ Company
Sales		
Variable expenses		
Income before interest		
Interest expense (fixed)		
Net Income		
Net income percent change		

(7)   Sales Decrease by _____ %

	_____ Company	_____ Company
Sales		
Variable expenses		
Income before interest		
Interest expense (fixed)		
Net Income		
Net income percent change		

(8)   Sales Decrease by _____ %

	_____ Company	_____ Company
Sales		
Variable expenses		
Income before interest		
Interest expense (fixed)		
Net Income		
Net income percent change		

(9) Analysis: _____

_____

_____

_____

_____

_____

_____

_____

_____

(1) Each Employee's FICA Withholdings for Social Security:

	Dale or Alli	Ted or Eve	Kate or Hong	Chas or Juan	Total
Maximum base					
Earned through _____					
Amt. subject to tax					
Earned this week					
Subject to tax					
Tax rate					
Social Security tax					

(2) Each Employee's FICA Withholdings for Medicare:

	Dale or Alli	Ted or Eve	Kate or Hong	Chas or Juan	Total
Earned this week					
Tax rate					
Medicare tax					

(3) Employer's FICA Taxes for Social Security:

	Dale or Alli	Ted or Eve	Kate or Hong	Chas or Juan	Total

(4) Employer's FICA Taxes for Medicare:

	Dale or Alli	Ted or Eve	Kate or Hong	Chas or Juan	Total

Chapter 11   Exercise 11-4A or 11-4B   Name _____
            (Continued)

(5) Employer's FUTA Taxes:

	Dale or Alli	Ted or Eve	Kate or Hong	Chas or Juan	Total
Maximum base					
Earned through _____					
Amt. subject to tax					
Earned this week					
Subject to tax					
Tax rate					
FUTA rate					

(6) Employer's SUTA Taxes:

	Dale or Alli	Ted or Eve	Kate or Hong	Chas or Juan	Total
Subject to tax					
Tax rate					
SUTA tax					

(7) Each Employee's Take-Home Pay:

	Dale or Alli	Ted or Eve	Kate or Hong	Chas or Juan	Total
Gross earnings					
Less:					
FICA Soc. Sec. tax					
FICA Medicare tax					
Withholding taxes					
Health Insurance					
Take-home pay					

(8) Employer's Total Payroll-Related Expense for Each Employee:

	Dale or Alli	Ted or Eve	Kate or Hong	Chas or Juan	Total
Gross earnings					
Plus:					
FICA Soc. Sec. tax					
FICA Medicare tax					
FUTA tax					
SUTA tax					
Health Insurance					
Pension contrib.					
Total payroll exp.					

(1)

GENERAL JOURNAL

Date		Account Titles and Explanation	P. R.	Debit	Credit

(2)

GENERAL JOURNAL

Date		Account Titles and Explanation	P. R.	Debit	Credit

GENERAL JOURNAL

Date	Account Titles and Explanation	P. R.	Debit	Credit

Work space:

GENERAL JOURNAL

Date	Account Titles and Explanation	P. R.	Debit	Credit
Continued from prior page				

Work Space:

(1) _____
_____
_____
_____
_____
_____

GENERAL JOURNAL

Date		Account Titles and Explanation	P. R.	Debit	Credit
(2)					
(3)					
(4)					

Work Space:

(a) **Correct Ending Balance of Cash and the Amount of the Omitted Check:** _____

_____
_____
_____
_____
_____
_____
_____
_____
_____
_____

(b) **Allowance for Doubtful Accounts:** _____

_____
_____
_____
_____
_____
_____

(c) **Depreciation Expense on the Truck:** _____

_____
_____
_____
_____
_____
_____

(d) **Depreciation Expense on the Equipment:** _____

_____
_____
_____
_____

(e) Adjusted Services Revenue and Unearned Services Revenue Balances:

_____
_____
_____
_____
_____
_____
_____
_____
_____
_____
_____
_____
_____
_____
_____
_____

(f) Warranty Expense and Estimated Warranty Liability:

_____
_____
_____
_____
_____
_____
_____
_____
_____
_____
_____

(g) Interest Payable and Interest Expense:

_____
_____
_____
_____
_____
_____
_____
_____
_____
_____
_____

Name _____

BUG-OFF EXTERMINATORS
December 31, 2005

Account Titles	Unadjusted Trial Balance		Adjustments		Adjusted Trial Balance	
	Dr.	Cr.	Dr.	Cr.	Dr.	Cr.
Cash						
Accounts Receivable						
Allowance for Doubtful Accounts						
Merchandise Inventory						
Trucks						
Accumulated Depreciation-Trucks						
Equipment						
Accum. Depreciation-Equipment						
Accounts Payable						
Estimated Warranty Liability						
Unearned Services Revenue						
Long-Term Notes Payable						
Interest Payable						
Common Stock						
Retained Earnings						
Extermination Services Revenue						
Interest Revenue						
Sales						
Cost of Goods Sold						
Depreciation Expense-Trucks						
Depreciation Expense-Equipment						
Wages Expense						
Interest Expense						
Rent Expense						
Bad Debts Expense						
Miscellaneous Expense						
Repairs Expense						
Utilities Expense						
Warranty Expense						
Totals						

GENERAL JOURNAL

Date	Account Titles and Explanation	P. R.	Debit	Credit

BUG-OFF EXTERMINATORS
Income Statement
For Year Ended December 31, 2005

BUG-OFF EXTERMINATORS
Statement of Owner's Equity
For Year Ended December 31, 2005

BUG-OFF EXTERMINATORS
Balance Sheet
December 31, 2005

(1) Times Interest Earned (2003): _____

_____

_____

Times Interest Earned (2002): _____

_____

_____

Times Interest Earned (2001): _____

_____

_____

Interpretation: _____

_____

_____

_____

(2) _____

_____

_____

_____

(3) Roll On: _____

_____

_____

_____

_____

_____

(1) Krispy Kreme's Times Interest Earned (Current Year): _____

_____

_____

     Krispy Kreme's Times Interest Earned (One Year Prior): _____

_____

_____

     Krispy Kreme's Times Interest Earned (Two Years Prior): _____

_____

_____

     Tastykake's Times Interest Earned (Current Year): _____

_____

_____

     Tastykake's Times Interest Earned (One Year Prior): _____

_____

_____

     Tastykake's Times Interest Earned (Two Years Prior): _____

_____

_____

(2)   Interpretation: _____

_____

_____

_____

_____

_____

(1) _____

_____

_____

_____

_____

_____

_____

_____

_____

(2) _____

_____

_____

_____

_____

_____

_____

_____

_____

_____

_____

MEMORANDUM

TO:
FROM:
SUBJECT:
DATE:

(1) _____

_____

_____

_____

(2) _____

_____

_____

_____

(3) _____

_____

_____

_____

_____

Teamwork in Action--BTN 11-6

(1) _____

_____

_____

_____

_____

Name _____

(2)

GENERAL JOURNAL

Date	Account Titles and Explanation	P. R.	Debit	Credit

(3) Team Discussion

(4)

GENERAL JOURNAL

Date	Account Titles and Explanation	P. R.	Debit	Credit

(5) Team Discussion

Chapter 11   *Business Week* Activity   *Name* _____
BTN 11-7

(1) _____
_____
_____
_____

(2) _____
_____
_____
_____
_____

(3) _____
_____
_____
_____
_____
_____

Times Interest Earned: _____

_____

_____

_____

_____

Part 2

Income Statement	
	Make Investment
Sales	
Depreciation	
Variable expenses	
Income before interest	
Interest expense	
Net income	

Times Interest Earned: _____

_____

_____

Part 3

Income Statement		
	No Investment	**Make Investment**
Sales		
Depreciation		
Variable expenses		
Income before interest		
Interest expense		
Net income		
Times Interest Earned:		

Income Statement		
	No Investment	Make Investment
Sales		
Depreciation		
Variable expenses		
Income before interest		
Interest expense		
Net income		
Times Interest Earned:		

Part 5

Income Statement		
	No Investment	Make Investment
Sales		
Depreciation		
Variable expenses		
Income before interest		
Interest expense		
Net income		
Times Interest Earned:		

Part 6

_____
_____
_____
_____
_____
_____
_____
_____
_____
_____
_____

_____
_____
_____
_____
_____
_____
_____
_____
_____
_____
_____
_____
_____
_____
_____
_____
_____
_____
_____
_____
_____

Global Decision--BTN 11-10

(1) Times Interest Earned	Current Year	One Year Prior

(2) _____
_____
_____
_____
_____
_____
_____
_____

Chapter 12   Quick Study 12-1   Name _____

(a) _____
_____
_____

(b) _____
_____
_____

Quick Study 12-2

	Share to Keeley	Share to Norton	Total
Net income			
Salary allowance:			
Keeley			
Norton			
Total salary allowances			
Balance of income			
Balance allocated:			
Keeley			
Norton			
Total allocated			
Balance of income			
Shares of the partners			

Quick Study 12-3

_____
_____
_____
_____
_____

Quick Study 12-4

_____
_____
_____
_____
_____

GENERAL JOURNAL

Date		Account Titles and Explanation	P. R.	Debit	Credit

Quick Study 12-6

GENERAL JOURNAL

Date		Account Titles and Explanation	P. R.	Debit	Credit

Quick Study 12-7

Name _____

Characteristic	General Partnerships
1. Life	
2. Owners' liability	
3. Legal status	
4. Tax status of income	
5. Owners' authority	
6. Ease of formation	
7. Transferability of ownership	
8. Ability to raise large amounts of capital	

Exercise 12-2
Part a

Recommended Organization: _____

_____

_____

_____

_____

Taxation Effects: _____

_____

_____

Advantages: _____

_____

_____

Recommended Organization: _____
_____
_____
_____
_____
_____

Taxation Effects:
_____
_____
_____

Advantages:
_____
_____
_____

Part c

Recommended Organization: _____
_____
_____
_____
_____
_____

Taxation Effects:
_____
_____

Advantages:
_____
_____
_____

(1)

GENERAL JOURNAL

Date	Account Titles and Explanation	P. R.	Debit	Credit

(2)

Capital account balances:	Abbey	Adams
Initial investment		
Withdrawals		
Share of income		
Ending balances		

Supporting calculations for (2)

_____
_____
_____
_____
_____
_____
_____
_____
_____
_____
_____
_____

Exercise 12-4

	Share to Cosmo	Share to Ellis	Total
(1)			
(2)			
(3)			

	Share to Cosmo	Share to Ellis	Total
(1)			
(2)			

Exercise 12-6

GENERAL JOURNAL

Date	Account Titles and Explanation	P. R.	Debit	Credit

(1)

GENERAL JOURNAL

Date	Account Titles and Explanation	P. R.	Debit	Credit

(2)

GENERAL JOURNAL

Date	Account Titles and Explanation	P. R.	Debit	Credit

(3)

GENERAL JOURNAL

Date	Account Titles and Explanation	P. R.	Debit	Credit

(1)

GENERAL JOURNAL

Date	Account Titles and Explanation	P. R.	Debit	Credit

(2)

GENERAL JOURNAL

Date	Account Titles and Explanation	P. R.	Debit	Credit

(3)

GENERAL JOURNAL

Date	Account Titles and Explanation	P. R.	Debit	Credit

Name _____

(1)

	Red	White	Blue	Total
Initial investments				
Allocation of all losses				
Capital balances				

(2)

GENERAL JOURNAL

Date	Account Titles and Explanation	P. R.	Debit	Credit

(3)

GENERAL JOURNAL

Date	Account Titles and Explanation	P. R.	Debit	Credit

Name _____

(a) Loss computation from selling assets: _____

_____
_____
_____
_____
_____
_____
_____
_____

(b) Loss allocation

	Tuttle	Ritter	Lee	Total
Capital balance before loss liquidation......................				
Allocation of loss:				
Capital balances after loss............				

(c) Liability to be paid: _____

_____
_____

Chapter 12   Exercise 12-11   Name _____

(a) Loss computation from selling assets: _____

_____
_____
_____
_____
_____
_____
_____

(b) Loss and deficit allocation:

	Tuttle	Ritter	Lee	Total
Capital balance before loss.........				
Allocation of loss:				
Capital balances after loss............				
Allocation of _____ deficit to				
Cash paid by each partner............				

(c) Liability to be paid: _____

_____

Exercise 12-12

_____
_____
_____
_____
_____
_____
_____
_____
_____
_____

GENERAL JOURNAL

Date	Account Titles and Explanation	P. R.	Debit	Credit
(1)				
(2)				
(3)				

Supporting calculations:

_____

_____

_____

_____

_____

_____

_____

_____

_____

_____

_____

_____

_____

_____

_____

_____

_____

Inc./Loss Sharing Plan	Year 1	
	Calculations	
(a)		
(b)		
(c)		
(d)		

Inc./Loss Sharing Plan	Year 2	
	Calculations	
(a)		
(b)		
(c)		
(d)		

Inc./Loss Sharing Plan	Year 3		
	Calculations		
(a)			
(b)			
(c)			
(d)			

Supporting Work Space:

Inc./Loss Sharing Plan	Calculations			Total
(a)				
(b)				
(c)				

				Total
PARTNERSHIP				
Statement of Partners' Equity				
For Year Ended December 31				
Beg. capital balances				
Plus:				
Owner investments				
Net Income:				
Salary allowances				
Interest allowances				
Balance allocated				
Total net income				
Total				
Less partners' withdrawals				
End. capital balances				

Part 3

GENERAL JOURNAL

Date	Account Titles and Explanation	P. R.	Debit	Credit

GENERAL JOURNAL

Date	Account Titles and Explanation	P. R.	Debit	Credit
(a)				
(b)				
(c)				
(d)				
(e)				

GENERAL JOURNAL

Date	Account Titles and Explanation	P. R.	Debit	Credit
(a)				
(b)				
(c)				

(1)

GENERAL JOURNAL

Date	Account Titles and Explanation	P. R.	Debit	Credit

(2)

GENERAL JOURNAL

Date	Account Titles and Explanation	P. R.	Debit	Credit

(3)

GENERAL JOURNAL

Date	Account Titles and Explanation	P. R.	Debit	Credit

(4)

GENERAL JOURNAL

Date	Account Titles and Explanation	P. R.	Debit	Credit

(1) _____

_____

_____

_____

_____

_____

_____

_____

(2)

GENERAL JOURNAL

Date	Account Titles and Explanation	P. R.	Debit	Credit

(3)

GENERAL JOURNAL

Date	Account Titles and Explanation	P. R.	Debit	Credit

(4) _____

_____

_____

_____

_____

_____

(1) _____
_____
_____
_____
_____
_____
_____
_____

(2) _____
_____
_____
_____
_____
_____
_____
_____
_____

(3) _____
_____
_____
_____
_____
_____
_____
_____
_____

Comparative Analysis--BTN 12-2

(1) _____
_____

(2) _____
_____
_____

(3) _____
_____

(4) _____
_____

(5) _____
_____
_____

(1) Income allocation per original agreement:

	Maben	Orlando	Clark	Total
Salary allowance				
Per patient charges				
Totals				

(2) Income allocation per Clark's proposal:

	Maben	Orlando	Clark	Total
Per patient charges				

(3)

_____
_____
_____
_____
_____
_____
_____
_____
_____
_____

STUDY NOTES

Organizations with Partnership Characteristics

Name _____

(1) _____

_____

_____

_____

_____

_____

(2) _____

_____

_____

_____

_____

_____

(3) _____

_____

_____

_____

_____

_____

_____

(4) _____

_____

_____

(1)

Income/Loss Sharing Plan	Calculations	Baker	Warner	Rice	Total
(a)					
(b)					
(c)					
(d)					

(2) Team members share solutions.

(3)

(1) _____
_____
_____

(2) _____
_____

(3) _____
_____
_____
_____
_____
_____

(4) _____
_____

(5) _____
_____
_____

Entrepreneurial Decision--BTN 12-8

(1) _____
_____
_____
_____
_____
_____
_____

(2) _____
_____
_____
_____

(3) _____
_____
_____
_____
_____
_____

(1) _____

_____

_____

(2) _____

_____

_____

(3) _____

_____

_____

_____

(4) _____

_____

(5) _____

_____

_____